ream Intruders

Riding Out the Storms of Life

GENE APPEL

STANDARD
PUBLISHING
Cincinnati, Ohio

Cover design by SchultzWard, Inc.

The Standard Publishing Company, Cincinnati, Ohio.
A division of Standex International Corporation.

00 99 98 97 96 95 94 93   5 4 3 2 1

Library of Congress Cataloging in Publication data:

Appel, Gene.
  Dream intruders : riding out the storms of life / Gene Appel.
    p. cm.
  ISBN 0-7847-0051-6
    1. Consolation.   2. Life.   I. Title.
  BV4905.2.A66   1993
  248.8'6—dc20   93-1342
                                                     CIP

Contents

When Visions Are Invaded 5

Accidents 7

Terminal Illness 21

You're Fired! 35

Prodigal Children 51

Bankruptcy 65

Divorce 81

Introduction

When Visions Are Invaded

I don't like dream intruders. I don't like to admit that life will never be exactly as I had dreamed and hoped it would be. A dream intruder is more than a temporary setback. It is an alteration of the planned course; a change of destination.

I got a new chair in my office a few years ago. My old chair was worn out—both arms on it were torn and the springs were shot. Its replacement was long overdue. So I had been looking forward to getting a new chair for a long time.

Our children's director went with me to pick it up, and we loaded it in the back of his pickup. On the way back to the church I said, "Roger, I know this will sound dumb, but I have looked forward to this day for four and a half years!"

He said, "Gene, that's just like you. You never let go of the vision."

He's right. By nature I am a visionary thinker. I don't let go of dreams and visions easily. That's the reason I especially struggle when a dream intruder comes into my life. I'll fight it to the bitter end. Dream intruders invade my visions and plunder my plans.

It would be nice if all of life were cloud-nine, a bowl of cherries, a walk in the park—but the real world is not like that. Accidents, terminal illness, being fired from a job, prodigal children, bankruptcy, and divorce weren't part of anybody's dreams. These intruders were not part of our plans.

This book is to reassure those of us who are meeting these dream intruders that we're not at the end. In fact, I'm learning that, when we feel as if we're at the end, that's often the point God is saying, "Finally, I've got your attention. I can do some of my best work in you right now." True life and true living begin only when our dream intruders bring death to our dreams and birth to the dreams that God has for us.

One of my goals in this book is to be real. I don't want to be trite and offer simple answers to complex hurts. I don't want to offer glib clichés and textbook formulas for dealing with dream intruders. Your hurts and your dream intruders are too real to be dealt with empirically.

We understand why Paul referred to our lives as jars of clay in 2 Corinthians 4. We are very fragile. We break easily. Sometimes jars are dropped and, though they can be glued back together, they bear some scars and cracks.

One of the difficult questions about dream intruders that I am not capable of answering in this book is why they come. When dream intruders come, we seize reason by the throat and demand answers to our questions: "Why me? Why now?" When answers don't come instantly, like a pack of gum from a vending machine, we are further perplexed.

I would just offer this observation: you will probably not understand the *why*s of most dream intruders for a long time. So rather than offer *why*s, I want to deal more with *what* and *how*. What do I do when a dream intruder comes? How do I get through it? May we hear the voice of God say to us as he said to Paul, "My grace is sufficient for you, for my power is made perfect in weakness" (2 Corinthians 12:9).

Dream Intruder #1

Accidents

The telephone rings in the middle of the night.

A child is late coming home.

Someone approaches you and says, "I think you better sit down."

They are experiences that unnerve us. We have a nagging fear of tragic accidents. The possibilities of potential accidents are limitless:

- A child is hit by a car.
- A motorcyclist goes off an embankment.
- A swimmer accidentally dives into the shallow end of a swimming pool.
- A machinist gets a part of his clothing grabbed by moving parts.
- A gun accidentally goes off while someone is hunting or cleaning.
- A drunk driver crosses lanes and drives head-on into another automobile.

- Someone trips and falls down some steps.
- Scaffolding collapses at a construction site.
- A boater inadvertently runs over a swimmer in the water.

Most of our fears are never realized. Fontaine sums them up maybe better than anyone when he says, "My life has been full of terrible misfortunes—most of which never happened." If you lived in slavery to the fear of the dream intruder of accidents, your life would be pretty limited in activity. You wouldn't ride in cars because they cause twenty percent of all fatal accidents. You wouldn't travel by air, rail, or water, where sixteen percent of all accidents take place. You couldn't even stay at home: seventeen percent of all accidents occur there. Why, by just walking down the street you'd be in danger because fourteen percent of all accidents happen to pedestrians. About the only safe place you could go would be church, where only one one-thousandth of one percent of all fatal accidents occur. So try to spend time at church whenever you can!

Maybe we need to begin this discussion by acknowledging the obvious.

Accidents Happen

I know this doesn't make accidents any easier to deal with, but we might as well accept the fact that accidents will happen in our lives. That doesn't take the pain out, and I'm not suggesting we casually blow them off just saying, "Well, that's life. Qué será será." But the fact still stands—accident happen.

Accidents Happen Throughout the Bible

In 2 Samuel 18 Absalom was riding his mule, and when the mule went under the thick branches of a large oak tree, Absalom's hair got caught in the tree. He was left hanging in midair, while the mule he was riding kept on going.

In Luke 13:4 Jesus referred to eighteen who died when the tower of Siloam fell on them.

In Acts 27 the apostle Paul and 275 other people were in a shipwreck on the Mediterranean Sea.

Acts 20 contains the story of Eutychus. He was attending a church service being held in a third-story room. Like many people today, Eutychus fell asleep in church. The tragic part is Eutychus was sitting in the ledge of a window. When he dozed off, he fell out the window and three stories down to his death. He was in that one one-thousandth of one percent!

Poor Eutychus. He falls asleep on one of the greatest preachers in history, the apostle Paul; he falls from a window and dies; and it's recorded in the Bible so people can read about it 2,000 years later. What a legacy! My mom asked me one time if I knew how Eutychus got his name.

I said, "No. How?"

She said, "'You'd-of-cussed' too if you'd have been killed falling three stories from a window in church!"

Now when Absalom got caught in the tree by his hair, when the tower of Siloam fell and killed eighteen people, when Paul's ship wrecked near the Island of Malta, and when Eutychus fell out of a window, we probably learn as much by what is not said in those texts as by what is said.

•No theological explanation is given for these accidents.

•There is no mention that the victims were being punished for anything.

They were accidents, just as the term implies. Accidents happen.

We've all had our fender benders. They happened so fast, we hardly knew what happened. Have you ever had to fill out an insurance form and write down in just a few words a summary of a traffic accident? The following explanations were published in a Toronto newspaper some years back:

•"Coming home, I drove into the wrong house and collided with a tree I don't have."

•"I thought my window was down, but found it was up when I put my hand through it."

- "I collided with a stationary truck coming the other way."
- "A pedestrian hit me and went under my car."
- "The guy was all over the road. I had to swerve a number of times before I hit him."
- "I pulled away from the side of the road, glanced at my mother-in-law, and headed over the embankment."
- "In my attempt to kill a fly, I drove into a telephone pole."
- "I had been driving my car for forty years when I fell asleep at the wheel and had an accident."
- "I was on my way to the doctor's with rear end trouble when my universal joint gave way, causing me to have an accident."

We've all had our little accidents. We all know accidents happen, but we wonder why they happen to "good" people. For instance, Eutychus was in church. That's one of the safest places he could be. Surely God wouldn't allow anything to happen to a guy in church! And why would God allow Paul to go through a shipwreck?

Jesus taught in Matthew 5:45 that the sun rises on the evil and the good, and rain falls on the righteous and the unrighteous. In other words, accidents are no respecter of persons. Accidents happen.

They *can* happen as a result of sin in one's life. If a person goes out and gets sloshed during the Super Bowl and then attempts to drive home after the game and hits a pedestrian, his sin has had a direct correlation to the accident. However, in Luke 13, Jesus teaches that accidents are not necessarily a result of sin in our lives. Let's look at the text more closely. Jesus asks, "Those eighteen who died when the tower in Siloam fell on them—do you think they were more guilty than all the others living in Jerusalem?" (Luke 13:4).

More guilty of what? Sin. Jesus was asking, "Do you think those who were killed when the tower fell on them were more sinful than everybody else in town?" This was an important question to raise because that was a common assumption. In that day they had people, as we have in ours, who taught that all human suffering is connected to sin; it's a punishment.

Were the eighteen more guilty of sin? Jesus answers the question with an exclamation mark: "I tell you, no!" (verse 5). He's not denying they were sinners. They were sinners just like everybody else in this world, but they weren't being punished for their sin. This was an accident. This is part of the fallout of living in a sinful fallen world.

We have no definite information about this tower that fell. We can only speculate. Maybe it fell because of poor workmanship. Maybe it fell because they had too many people in it. Maybe it was under construction and something wasn't braced properly. Maybe it was old and had deteriorated until it finally collapsed.

Whatever the reason, Jesus' point was that it wasn't a punishment on those who died. If it had been a punishment for sin, everybody in Jerusalem would have died with them!

When an accident strikes, I know people who say, "God must be getting me for something. There must be something bad in my life or this wouldn't have happened." Well, we've all got some bad things in our lives. We've all made mistakes. But we are talking about accidents: unforeseen, undesigned mishaps.

Accidents happen, and when they do, suddenly everything changes. It happened in our family. A number of years ago my uncle Johnny and Aunt Virginia loaded up their car with their five children, another aunt, and her three children. Eleven people were in the automobile. Uncle Johnny had been drinking, and he drove head-on into another automobile. Johnny and Virginia were killed, leaving five parentless young children behind.

An accident like that changes everything for the lives of many people. My grandparents, who had already raised their four children, took the three oldest children and raised them. The oldest one was fourteen. Another aunt and uncle adopted the youngest daughter, who was just a baby at the time. My Mom and Dad adopted Mike, who was four years old.

Everything changed. The lives of four family units were totally turned around. These five brothers and sisters never grew up as brothers and sisters. But I'll tell you something, even though everything changed and we have this terrible tragedy in our memory, life went on for everybody. I don't want you to misunderstand me. Not for a second am I happy about this tragedy! But I am very thankful for my brother Mike, whom I probably would have only known as a distant cousin under other circumstances. I treasure him. He means everything to me.

So accidents happen. And when they happen, you find out something vital about yourself.

Accidents Reveal Your Character

One test of your faith is how you handle a crisis. Anybody can be a Christian when things are going great, when all our prayers are being answered the way we ask them, when we're in good health, when our income is rising. It's easy to be a Christian at times like that. The test of our faith is when problems come—when accidents hit. Character is not made in a crisis, but it is revealed in a crisis. Accidents will demonstrate your character, not make your character. Your character is made in the day-to-day, mundane, trivial things of life—the routine. Character is revealed when your life encounters a shipwreck.

In Acts 27 Paul was being taken prisoner by ship to Rome. On the way, the 276 people on board found themselves in the midst of hurricane-force winds that drove them out on the sea for days. During this uncertain time, character was revealed.

The Sailors' Reaction

The sailors' reaction reminds us of some of our typical responses in the midst of a crisis. First, they quit trying to sail and just allowed the ship to drift. When a crisis hits, we sometimes feel the best thing to do is just to let the circumstances carry us wherever we end up. This is no time to worry about our intended destination; the important thing is just to survive! We'll regroup after the storm.

Next, the sailors started throwing everything they could get their hands on overboard. It was an attempt to lighten the load so the ship would ride higher on the water during the storm. Sometimes in a crisis we realize that some of the things we had thought were important are not so important after all.

But even after these valiant efforts to handle things on their own, the Bible says they gave up all hope of being saved. Ultimately, the sailors demonstrated their character. They had forgotten God was in control, and even in a crisis, God has a plan.

Paul's Reaction

Now in 180-degree contrast to the reaction of the sailors was Paul. In the midst of the crisis he was calm, confident, and courageous. Nothing seemed to phase his rock-solid faith. His character emerged in at least three ways.

First, *Paul planted himself on the rock.* One of the safest things to do when the storms of life blow is to anchor yourself firmly to the Lord. Often when people encounter a life-changing storm, they begin to look for what they can change rather than what needs to remain consistent. We don't need more change, like a change in job, a change in location, a change in scenery. We need stability. Paul stood on the rock of the Lord and said, "Keep your courage, men. I've got faith."

Second, *he remembered God was with him.* In the midst of the storm Paul said, "Last night an angel of the God whose I am and whom I serve stood beside me" (Acts 27:23). Paul had discovered the Lord was with him when things were going well in life, and he knew God would be with him in the face of this tragedy.

We may think God is a million miles away and can't see us, but he's always with the Christian. He has said, "Never will I leave you; never will I forsake you" (Hebrews 13:5). "And surely I am with you always" (Matthew 28:20). "And I will ask the Father, and he will give you another Counselor to be with you forever—the Spirit of truth" (John 14:16, 17). Over and over the Bible says wherever you are, God is right there with you.

Third, *Paul relied on the promises of God.* Paul told the men, "So keep up your courage, men, for I have faith in God that it will happen just as he told me" (Acts 27:25). Paul believed and remembered the promises of God.

In his book, *A Future and a Hope,* Lloyd Ogilvie writes of a trip to Scotland where he spent several weeks researching everything he could find on the subject of hope. He completed his research for the book, but hadn't actually started to write it. Searching for ideas on how better to communicate the concept of hope to others, one rainy evening on the rugged northwestern coastline, Ogilvie went hiking to a favorite remote rock on the seashore. The closer he got, the faster he ran, vaulting from boulder to boulder. One more spring was all he needed to reach the top.

Then, as he moved his left leg for that final leap, his right foot slipped. In this freak accident he skidded, fell between boulders, broke his leg in six places, badly damaged the knee and ligaments around it, and was knocked unconscious.

After regaining consciousness, he realized he was miles from anyone and hadn't told anybody where he was going, so he wouldn't be missed till morning. He knew, however, that he couldn't live through the cool night if he stayed there. In excruciating pain, he began pulling himself back on his hands. He called out for help, but no one heard. Over rocks, through fields full of sheep dung, he made his way, deeply cutting his hands. When he reached a point where he couldn't move another inch, this man who was going to write a book on hope recalled the promises of God. One in particular came to mind that he had memorized from Jeremiah 29:11-13:

"For I know the thoughts that I think toward you, saith the Lord, thoughts of peace and not of evil, to give you a future and a hope. Then you will call up Me and go and pray to me, and I will listen to you. And you will seek Me and find Me, when you search for Me with all your heart" (NKJV).

He realized at that moment that the Lord didn't just *give* hope, but the Lord *was* his hope; the Lord was his future.

In time, he was found and began the long convalescence to being functional again. His life was changed forever. One slip on a rock had not only crushed his leg, it had smashed all his plans. Yet he remembered the promises of God.

Character is revealed in times of crisis.

An Opportunity for Further Personal Growth

Accidents happen, and accidents reveal our character. In addition, accidents provide an opportunity for personal growth that probably would never occur in any other way.

An accident has a way of helping us see for whom and for what we have been living. We are able to gain a new perspective on life and discover some blind spots. We certainly shouldn't pray for accidents to come just so we can experience further growth! But when they do come, if we don't grow through them, this dream intruder will destroy us.

There's an old poem that closes with the line: "It's not the gale, but the set of the sail, that determines which way you go." In Luke 13, Jesus connected the accidental death of the eighteen killed when the tower of Siloam fell on them to a parable for the living. It's almost as if Jesus was saying, "Yes, this accident happened to them, but what about you? Would you be prepared for such an accident?"

Then he told this parable:

A man had a fig tree, planted in his vineyard, and he went to look for fruit on it, but did not find any. So he said to the man who took care of the vineyard, "For three years now I've been coming to look for fruit on this fig tree and haven't found any. Cut it down! Why should it use up the soil?"

"Sir," the man replied, "leave it alone for one more year, and I'll dig around it and fertilize it. If it bears fruit next year, fine! If not, then cut it down" (Luke 13:6-9).

This fig tree hadn't been producing fruit for three years. The owner wanted to cut it down, but the gardener said, "Let me fertilize it and turn up the soil, and let's give it one more shot. If it doesn't produce fruit this next year, then we'll cut it down."

You see, the people to whom Jesus told this parable could just as easily have been taken in an accidental death as the eighteen were, but they were spared. What, Jesus wanted to know, were they going to do with the opportunity they had? Are there lessons they could learn from the death of the eighteen?

We see in this parable that the message of Christianity is all about a second chance. This fig tree was given another chance. And these people were being given a chance to turn to Jesus Christ. Jesus said, "Unless you repent, you too will all perish" (Luke 13:3). The message of the Christian faith is, "You need another chance. All people are sinners, but Jesus Christ died and paid the penalty in your place. If you'll appropriate the blood of Jesus Christ as the penalty for your sin, you can have a second chance!"

Maybe you are really struggling as you read these words because you caused an accident. You wonder, "How can I ever forgive myself? How can I ever be forgiven?" Maybe it was unintentional, but you are dogged with guilt. You didn't see the child coming on the bike. You had had too much to drink. You didn't know the gun was loaded. You fell asleep at the wheel. The brakes just didn't work when you applied them. The message of this parable is that Jesus wants to give you a second chance. He can forgive you.

In the Old Testament God established "cities of refuge" where people who had accidentally killed somebody could go and be protected. This was a place of protection in case a person shoved somebody and unintentionally killed him. It was a place of safety for any kind of accidental death, so those who had accidentally killed someone could be protected from an avenger. It's almost as if God was saying, "I know accidents happen. I'll forgive you. I will provide a refuge of safety for you. Even if others don't accept or forgive, I will."

Someone sent me a card one time with a giraffe on the cover. His head was way up in a tree, and he was talking with a bird. The cover said, "Jesus loves you!" On the inside it said, "And it never hurts to have friends in high places." Jesus does love you, and he wants to give you a second chance.

While we learn through this parable that we all can have a second chance, we also learn there is a final chance. The tree would have its chance, but it eventually would be cut down. Jesus taught you don't know when you may have your final chance to get right with the Lord, but one day will be your last. Maybe the accident of another, or even your own, helps you realize how fragile life is and how close we all are from entering eternity. Jesus is saying, "Let me give you a second chance."

God can bring about good even in the face of accidents, in the face of loss of limbs, in the face of a coma, in the face of paralysis. Joni EarecksonTada experienced it on a day in 1967 when she dived from a little raft in the Chesapeake Bay. Her head struck a rock in the shallow waters, which she thought were deep. An athletic, coordinated, beautiful girl became a paralytic with no feeling from her neck down—as she remains to this day.

Think of being paralyzed. How many activities would drastically change for you? Think of hearing words like, "I'm sorry. The surgery didn't take. We've done all we can. You'll never walk again." I don't think there's a one of us who wouldn't submerge into a period of depression and disillusionment if that were us, at least for a while. And she did.

Yet Joni Eareckson found this dream intruder could be the beginning of new dreams. Through her incredible commitment to Christ, she developed an art ministry of drawing with her teeth. She has a syndicated radio program and a writing ministry. She has single-handedly done more to make churches aware of the special needs of the handicapped than anyone in history! She found a future and a hope. I think her words can be a great comfort to everyone who has faced the futile feelings an accident can bring. She writes:

"Have faith, Joni...one day it will all be better."

I can't tell you how many times I heard words like those from sad-faced friends who clung to the guardrail of my hospital bed when I was first injured.

"Have faith, Joni...faith will see you through to the end."

Boy that sounded morbid to me.

I could never be comforted by words like those. They always left me with a feeling that nothing much was *really* going to change. My paralysis was still to be a prison, and faith—a kind of hopeful, wistful longing—was only a religious warm fuzzy to cheer me until a faraway, future day when everything would "make sense."

If being a woman of great faith meant sitting around in my wheelchair longing for pie in the sky I wanted no part of it.

What a colossal misunderstanding!

Faith, as the Bible defines it, is present-tense action. It's taking God's promises and acting on them *today...*

Somewhere along the line...I began to realize that faith means being sure of what we hope for...*now*. It means knowing something is real, *this moment*...even when you don't see it.

When I started living like this, I suddenly understood I could get a jump-start on heaven. I could start living for eternity today. I could have confidence that God had His busy fingers working on me moment by moment, even though I couldn't see or feel them.

Great faith isn't the ability to believe long and far into the misty future. It's simply taking God at His word and taking the next step."[1]

Faith is how you will make it, too. Faith that trusts God today. Accidents happen. You'll find out your true character when they do, but it will also be a time that will present a great opportunity for personal growth. Faith is taking God at his word.

A minister was called to the home of a woman whose only son had been killed in a tragic accident. As the preacher came to the house, the distraught mother came running to confront him. "Where was your God when my son died?" she asked. Quietly the minister responded, "The same place he was when his own Son died."

Friend, God knows all about pain. He experienced the pain of the cross so that we could have the ultimate victory over our dream intruders. God can bring good, even out of suffering. God will be victorious in the end.

As Maltbie Babcock put it:

This is my Father's world.
O let me ne'er forget
That though the wrong seems oft so strong,
God is the Ruler yet!

Will you take God at his word? Is he the ruler of your life? Would you like him to be? What are you waiting for?

Questions for Discussion

1. What do you think of the author's assertion that we need to start by simply accepting the fact that "accidents happen"? In what way, if any, does that help you deal with the fact of accidents in your life?

[1]Excerpted by permission from the book *Glorious Intruder*, Joni Eareckson Tada. Questar Publishers/Multnomah Books, ©1989, Multnomah.

2. The author says accidents *can* happen as a result of sin in one's life. In what ways can recognizing this fact be helpful in dealing with an accident? What dangers are present in trying too hard to determine what sin may have caused an accident?

3. Imagine you were on the ship with Paul. (Read Acts 27.) You saw no angels reassuring you of safety. How do you think you would have reacted? Why do you think you would have reacted in this way?

4. How can one build his character so that an accident will reveal positive traits instead of negative ones? Can this be done alone, or is help from others required? If the latter, who can provide this help?

5. The author says the sailors (Acts 27) "had forgotten God was in control, and even in crisis, God has a plan." Do you think this affirmation of God's sovereignty contradicts the earlier assertion that "accidents happen"? Why or why not?

6. The author cites Lloyd Ogilvie's accident and says, "He realized . . . that the Lord didn't just *give* hope, but the Lord *was* his hope." What difference do you see between the idea that the Lord *gives* hope and the Lord *is* one's hope?

7. Can you remember an accident that produced personal growth in your life? Do you think the same growth would have occurred without the accident's happening? Why or why not?

8. Joni Erickson Tada is quoted as saying faith is "simply taking God at His word." Would you agree? Why or why not? How does faith help you deal with accidents?

9. How would you have answered the mother who said, "Where was your God when my son died?" What advice or counsel would you give a friend today who was trying to cope with the result of an accident in her life?

Dream Intruder #2

Terminal Illness

No matter how many times I've been with families through the dream intruder of a terminal illness, through the long days of sickness, through the praying beside a hospital bed, through the cries of hopelessness wondering whether God is hearing their cries for help, this is one area of my ministry that I never get used to.

I've never been able to get a lock on the right comforting words. I've never figured out how to say just the right thing to lift the spirits of a hurting daughter or son. I'm not sure I can begin to feel the pain of a husband or wife who sits by the bed of his mate, with whom he has shared so many memories.

Though I've had the opportunity to minister in these types of situations many times, it never gets any easier. I just kind of plod through. Maybe that's all we can do. So in this chapter I simply want to help you understand this difficult period in life and why it evokes some of the emotions, feelings, and pain it does. Maybe you can find some comfort in knowing that your responses in terminal illness are not out of the ordinary, and what you're feeling and experiencing has been shared by many other people.

Sickness is an issue that runs throughout the pages of Scripture. When Jesus walked the earth, his concern for the sick was so extensive that almost one fifth of the Gospels is devoted to healing. Biblical illnesses that potentially led to death—except for a miracle—included the following:

- Fever, like the one Simon Peter's mother-in-law had in Matthew 8.
- Pestilence, like the one described in 2 Samuel 24, which killed 70,000 people in three days.
- Plagues and worms.

Terminal illness—that is, an illness by which, barring a miracle, death is imminent—has struck every period in history. Some historians say that the Black Death, which swept through Europe in the fourteenth century, killed as much as one third of the population! Those who survived must have spent most of their days burying the dead and wondering who was going to be next.

The good news of the twentieth century has been the retreat of many of the dreaded diseases. Polio, typhoid, diphtheria, and small pox have all but disappeared. Yet even with all of the breakthroughs in medicine, we still face many illnesses that have no sure cure. Some of them ravage a body quickly. Others work over a long course of time, slowly debilitating and deteriorating the body.

Too many times we have seen the ravage of cancer throughout the body of someone we love. Alzheimer's disease is so painful for loved ones to endure as they watch someone deteriorate to a point the person doesn't even know them or seem like the same person they have known and loved. AIDS research continues at a rapid pace, but no cure is in sight. Blood clots, tumors, tired body organs, and even pneumonia can take the life of a loved one so quickly at times. There are illnesses that occur years later because of a birth defect. Sometimes an illness rages internally throughout a person's life and there is no clue of a problem until another life is claimed.

I want to deal with the dream intruder of terminal illness by looking at it in three stages: before the illness, during the illness, and after the illness. Every one of us is living in one of these three stages right now!

Before the Illness

Maybe you've never had to face firsthand a terminal illness in someone close to you, but you know it's only a matter of time. It may be someone you love very much. It may even be you.

I think one of the best things all of us can do to prepare for a terminal illness is to face the reality of death.

Face the Reality of Death

Hebrews 9:27 tells us that "man is destined to die once, and after that to face judgment."

George Bernard Shaw wrote, "The statistics on death are quite impressive. One out of every one people dies."

Our generation has made use of every technological means to try to beat death. For instance, remarkable progress has been made in transplanting vital body organs. Lives that, twenty years ago, would be over are now being extended with heart, kidney, and liver transplants. Researchers are studying the possibility of extending life through transplants of even the lungs and the brain. But even though life may be prolonged through spare parts, we all know that death will ultimately be faced by all of us.

We have trouble coming to grips with the reality of death. We don't talk about death in front of children—or ever if we can help it! Since 1965, when Robert Ettinger published *The Prospect of Immortality,* the public has become aware of the idea of cryonics—the quick freezing of one who has died with the hope that he can be revived in the future when a cure for his illness is found. More and more people are having this done.

English essayist J.B. Priestly said, "Mankind is frightened by the mere word 'death,' and nowhere more so than in America. At dinner parties there I have brought up the question of death just to study the stunned reaction. Most people switched off the subject as if they were switching channels."

The reality that few of us like to admit is that we're all terminally ill. If nothing else, old age is a disease that will eventually take all of us. Once you reach the age of twenty-two, the new cells your body produces to replace the dying ones are not as good as they ones they replace. From that point on there is decreasing muscular strength, gradually defective eyesight, hearing, etc. In other words, it's all downhill from twenty-two!

One of the best things all of us can do that will prepare us before an illness hits is to admit our own mortality—we are going to die. William Randolph Hearst, the multi-millionaire publisher, would not permit the word *death* ever to be mentioned in his presence. When actor Henry Fonda died, the family didn't want any service in his honor because they didn't want to think about him as being dead.

I think a big problem of the "mid-life crisis" is not just that a person's body begins to slow down or he realizes he's not going to reach his financial goals. I think the problem is he realizes his life is going to end. If there's a middle, there has to be an end. And the realizes he is getting closer to the end all the time.

I am not saying people should be obsessed with the thought of their own death, but occasionally they do need to talk it over with people who are close to them. Sometimes people try to talk about death, but they can't say, "I'm going to die." They say things like, "I might not always be here," or, "When you get back, if I'm not here. . . ." We ought to be able to say frankly, "Hey, when I die, there are certain things I want you to be aware of." Jesus told his disciples he was going to go up to Jerusalem and be handed over to his enemies and be killed (cf. Luke 18:31-33). Likewise, we need to say on occasion to those closest to us, "This is the way I'd like matters to be handled when I die." That makes it so much easier for the family to adjust, and it helps us to confront our own mortality.

For many years, my dad kept a sealed updated letter on file that was addressed, "To the family of L.H. Appel in case of his death." In it he wrote out specific instructions for the funeral: where it should be held; who should preach; Scripture to be used; who should sing; pall bearers; and where important papers and documents could be found. When he died unexpectedly at the age of fifty-two, it made it so much easier on us as a family that he had been willing to face the reality of death long before it ever happened.

Prepare for What Comes After Death

Before an illness hits, beyond facing the reality of death, we need to prepare for what comes afterwards. In John, chapter 11, we find the story of the death of Lazarus. Lazarus and his sisters, Mary and Martha, lived in the town of Bethany. They were close personal friends with Jesus.

While Jesus was in Perea (the area east of the Jordan River), he received word that Lazarus had been afflicted with a terminal illness. Verse 3 says, "The sisters sent word to Jesus, 'Lord, the one you love is sick.'" Just that wording gives us a clue to the closeness of the friendship that had developed between Jesus and Lazarus.

But it took a few days for Jesus to get back to Bethany, and on his arrival Jesus discovered that Lazarus had already been in the tomb for four days. Martha went out to meet Jesus. Her conversation with Jesus reveals much about the faith of this family.

"Jesus said to her, 'Your brother will rise again.'

"Martha answered, 'I know he will rise again in the resurrection at the last day'" (John 11:23, 24). Notice that here was a family member who was grieving—but grieving with hope.

The Bible doesn't say that believers don't grieve, but that we don't grieve "as those who have no hope" (1 Thessalonians 4:13). Martha knew her brother was going to rise again. What gave her that hope? It was the relationship that her brother had established with Jesus Christ before he died.

> Jesus said to her, "I am the resurrection and the life. He who believes in me will live, even though he dies; and whoever lives and believes in me will never die. Do you believe this?"
> "Yes, Lord," she told him, "I believe that you are the Christ, the Son of God who was to come into the world" (John 11:25-27).

An ongoing relationship with Jesus Christ prepares people at any time for an untimely death. Jesus said, "Those who believe in me, even though they die, will live. In fact, they will never die." He put it another way in John 3:16, "For God so loved the world that he gave his one and only Son, that whoever believes in him shall not perish but have eternal life."

No doubt someone reading these words is in the midst of a serious illness right now. It may or may not be terminal, but you are in the fight of your life. The gravity of the situation has forced you, for the first time in your life, to begin thinking seriously about eternity and what comes after death. If I could tell you anything, I would tell you to do what Lazarus did: develop a personal relationship with Jesus Christ. Only the one who had power to rise from the dead himself can give you the power to rise from the dead. And that's Jesus!

Before an illness we need to face the reality of death and then prepare spiritually for what comes after death.

During the Illness

Perhaps you are in the throes of a terminal illness right now. Or perhaps a loved one is. Either way, you're not sure of what you're feeling. The fruit basket of your life has been turned upside down.

The Patient

Try to understand what the terminally ill patient is going through at the time of an illness. One cancer patient says, "The earth stood still the day my doctor told me I had cancer. I remember the walls in my room were sickly pink. It was an emotional shock to me and my family unlike any other we had experienced. I couldn't think straight."[2]

Dr. Elisabeth Kubler-Ross,[3] a pioneer in the study of the process of dying, says the terminally ill patient ordinarily goes through five stages of dealing with the illness. Not everyone experiences every stage or in the same order, and the duration of each may vary, but the following emotions are typical.

The first reaction is *denial*. The patient refuses to believe the diagnosis. "It must be someone else. You must have read the wrong Xrays." One physician reports that her patients have partial deafness when she tries to describe their illnesses. After years of working with seriously ill patients, she assumes that a patient will hear only one third of what she says about his or her condition.

Denial may help us absorb bad news slowly, but it can also cause problems. It may even make some people delay treatment until a disease is no longer curable. "If I deny it, it will go away."

The second reaction moves from denial to *anger and bitterness*. A patient is likely to start blaming God: "Why would God allow this to happen to me if he really loved me?—if there really is a God!" She may get angry at family or the hospital staff. From her perspective, it's like a terrible disease reaches out arbitrarily and says, "Tag! You're it!"

One minister experienced in serving the sick said, "Always remember: it's hard to act nice when you feel terrible."

[2]Batsell Barret Baxter, et. al., *Anchors in Troubled Waters* (Grand Rapids: Baker, 1981), p.111.

[3]*On Death and Dying* (New York: Macmillan, 1969).

In the third stage the patient begins *bargaining.* Do you remember the movie *The End* with Burt Reynolds and Dom Delouise? Burt Reynolds was going to commit suicide by swimming out in the ocean and just letting the currents take him under. But after swimming out a long way, he became afraid of death and decided he wanted to live after all. However, by this time he was so far from the shoreline that he didn't know if he had enough strength to make it back. So he started bargaining with God. He said things like, "Lord, if you'll let me live, I'll give 60% of everything I make for the rest of my life." But then he got a little closer to shore and he said, "Lord, I'll give you 50% of everything I ever make if you help me make it back." The closer he got, the less he was willing to give God. Finally, when he was almost back to shore, he said something like, "Well, maybe I didn't mean I'd give you anything, but I'll be real grateful!"

When people get in a tight spot, they start bargaining with God. A terminally ill patient might say, "God, if you'll only give me a few more months, I'll be a different person."

The terminally ill patient may then move to *depression.* Job did. He said, "What I feared has come upon me; what I dreaded has happened to me. I have no peace, no quietness; I have no rest, but only turmoil" (Job 3:25, 26).

All of us feel that way sometimes. I got a card from my sister-in-law once that pictured a car taking off for a drive down the road. It said, "Whenever life begins to overwhelm me, I take a drive in the country to relax...." When I opened it up, it said, "...and now I'm 2600 miles from home!"

During depression, patients often look back and question the value of the life they've lived. They wonder, "What have I accomplished? What have I done that is significant?"

Finally, in the last stage, after this physically, emotionally, and spiritually painful journey, the patient reaches *acceptance.* Gradually there comes that time when the patient is able to pray the prayer of serenity: "Lord, grant me the serenity to accept the things I cannot change, the courage to change the things I can, and the wisdom to know the difference."

When a patient reaches this point, he will probably want to talk, so you need to let him. I've been with terminally ill people who knew they were going to die and wanted to talk with family members about it, but their family would interrupt them and say, "Oh, Mom, don't talk like that. You're not going to die. You'll outlive us all!" But everybody knows that's not true, and that mother is denied the privilege of saying what needs to be said and what others need to hear. She is on a journey through the valley of the shadow of death, and now she has reached the point whre she fears no evil. She knows God's rod and staff are there to comfort her. She is ready to talk to her family about how, through Christ, she is going to dwell in the house of the Lord forever!

The Family

Not only does the patient suffer, but the family experiences incredible pain, anguish, and pressure. Even though Mary and Martha knew their brother would live again, his sickness and subsequent death had been very hard on them. That's the reason they had sent word to Jesus to come quickly. They had hoped something could be done before his sickness took him.

Sometimes a terminal illness in a family can bring the family closer together. In many other cases it has put family members at each other's throats. There is considerable strain when a member of the family is terminally ill. The longer the illness is stretched out, the greater the emotional stress becomes on the family. Eventually somebody just breaks.

I've seen families split because they can't agree on how much to tell Mom or Dad, who lies dying in the hospital bed. They're afraid the loved one will panic or become depressed if he is told the truth. Others fear the patient will become angry if he is not told and finds out the truth later. While there is this disagreement in the family, the patient suffers more because he is not getting the support he needs.

Communication is essential between the patient and family regarding the disease and the treatment plan. The patient usually discovers the seriousness of his sickness even if he is never told. The sooner there is open communication between the patient and his family regarding the illness, the better the patient's attitude will be. It's when family members disagree about these matters that the strife can come.

I know it's tough to keep that perspective, because you are going through all of your own hurts. You keep trying to blame somebody for this frustrating dream intruder. But I want to encourage you during this time of illness—which may last days, weeks, months, or years—to take the high road.

- Unite the family.
- Demonstrate the spiritual fruit of patience, longsuffering, kindness, gentleness, love, and peace.
- Don't let your own needs blind you of the needs of the patient, but don't ignore your needs either. Talk about them with a close friend.

After the Illness

Finally it comes: the day of the last good-bye, the last kiss, the last "I love you." Now those who are left behind who have been giving their attention to the patient, in a sense become patients themselves. Everyday they live with the reminder that life will never again be as it was.

Many have found it helpful to work through their feelings during grief by writing them down. It was C.S. Lewis who wrote: "Her absence is like the sky, spread over everything." William Armstrong wrote, "Back in the house I moved on leaden feet from chore to chore." Ada Campbell Rose wrote: "The mantle of grief falls on every hour of the days and covers me while I sleep. Will it ever go away?"

A little book I have found helpful for understanding and dealing with grief is called *Good Grief*. It's not by Charlie Brown, but by Granger Westberg.[4] It takes less than an hour

[4]Granger Westberg, *Good Grief* (Philadelphia: Fortress Press, 1964).

to read, but it's one of the most helpful books I know. It identifies common stages of grief. These stages are experienced to some degree whenever you face any dream intruder, whether it's an accident, death, being fired, or divorce. Everyone doesn't experience all the stages nor go through them in the same order, and it's possible to experience several stages at one time. But we all grieve.

At the outset you feel *shock*. This may last a few hours or a few days. Often a grieving mate is seen at a funeral and people will say, "She has such a peace!" Yet the truth may be that she is in shock, kind of a temporary anesthesia that helps her get ready to move to the next stage of grief.

Then most move to a time of *emotional release.* The significance of the loss begins to hit. Many men struggle through this point because they are afraid to show tears. The "manly" thing to do is choke the tears back, which may inhibit the grieving process. They need to get it out.

Eventually there comes a feeling of *depression and isolation.* I want you to remember those days will pass. Dark days do not last forever. Psalm 30:5 reminds us, "Weeping may remain for a night, but rejoicing comes in the morning."

Some people begin to experience *physical problems* while they're grieving. Others go through a state of *panic* because they can think of nothing but the loss. Another common stage is feeling a sense of *guilt* about the loss. Maybe you feel guilty about something you did or did not do for the deceased. Prayer will be a great release for your guilt. First John 1:9 reminds us, "If we confess our sins, he is faithful and just and will forgive us our sins and purify us from all unrighteousness." But some have a neurotic guilt—guilt that is not deserved. A daughter stayed by her mother's bedside in the hospital for days and days, but finally, under the doctor's orders, went home and got some sleep. But that turned out to be the night her mother died, and now she cannot forgive herself for not being there when it happened. She builds up this situation way out of proportion. Unhealthy guilt needs to be talked out with someone, or it may block a person's full recovery.

A period of *anger and resentment* is common. As people move out of depression, they express strong feelings of anger and are often critical of everything and everyone who was related to the loss. The doctor shouldn't have operated—or he should have. No matter what he did, it was wrong.

There is often a *resistance to returning to usual activities.* People are afraid that, if they get back to normal activities, everyone will forget the tragedy. They want somebody to keep the memory alive. You can help people through this stage by talking about their lost loved one from time to time. Remember a good time, a laugh, a kiss. It may bring a tear to their eye, but they'll be glad you remember.

As a person works through these stages, gradually *hope* comes through. The person finds he can't put off going forward with a meaningful life forever.

Finally you get back into *reality.* I don't want to say, "You become your old self again." When you go through a significant grief experience, you come out of it a different person. You eventually realize, though your loss has been great, not everything has been taken from you. There is much in life that still is good.

Years ago the Flying Wallenda family experienced a tragedy while performing at a circus. As they attempted to perform a difficult formation on the high wire, two members of the family were killed and two others were injured for life. The Wallendas stopped their performances. They withdrew and became cautious, which is a normal response. In time, however, they said they would get back up on the wire. In fact, they would perform the very act that had led to the tragedy. The day came for the comeback. While people anxiously waited in the stands, the Wallendas successfully reconstructed their human pyramid on the high wire. Afterward, reporters descended on them. "Why did you try this act after the tragedy of a few years ago?" The senior member of the family replied, "To be on the wire is life. All else is waiting."

Do you need to get back out on the wire and experience life again? Isn't it about time? Do you want to know how? King David wrote: "Even though I walk through the valley of the shadow of death, I will not be afraid, for you are with me; your rod and your staff, they comfort me" (Psalm 23:4).

God really does help you through. Martha was able to face the reality of the loss of her brother because of her faith in Jesus. She confidently said, "I know he will rise again."

Then Jesus did something miraculous. Going to the grave of his friend, where he was moved to tears, he had the stone rolled away. Then he called out in a loud voice, "Lazarus, come out!" And Lazarus rose from the dead (John 11:43, 44).

When Jesus demonstrated his power over death by raising Lazarus from the dead, he also demonstrated that he has the power to raise you and he has the power to raise your loved ones. The key is faith in Jesus Christ. Jesus said, "He who believes in me will live, even though he dies" (John 11:25).

We all have a terminal disease. It is called sin. It is a disease that leads to death. The Bible says the wages of sin is death—that's physical death and spiritual death. But the Bible also says that the free gift of God is eternal life through Jesus Christ our Lord.

Eternal life is a gift that has to be received. Have you accepted it? When you do, the hope of the resurrection will be yours. And when you're gone, your family will be able to hear you say:

> Don't grieve for me, for now I'm free.
> I'm following the path God has laid, you see.
> I took His hand when I heard His call;
> I turned my back and left it all.
>
> I could not stay another day
> To laugh, to love, to work, or play.
> Tasks left undone must stay that way.
> I found the peace at the close of the day.
>
> If my parting has left a void,
> Then fill it with remembered joys.
> A friendship shared, a laugh, a kiss.
> Oh yes, these things I too will miss.

Be not burdened with times of sorrow.
I wish you the sunshine of tomorrow.
My life's been full, I savored much.
Good friends, good times, a loved one's touch.

Perhaps my time seemed all too brief.
Don't lengthen it now with undue grief.
Lift up your hearts and peace to thee.
God wanted me now; He set me free.[5]

Questions for Discussion

1. The author says, "Every one of us is living in one of these three stages [of terminal illness] right now." How does realizing that fact change your perspective on life?
2. Why do you think we have such a hard time coming to grips with death?
3. Is our culture's reluctance to face death a help or a hindrance for sharing the gospel? What makes you think so?
4. Compare Elisabeth Kubler-Ross's stages of grief with Granger Westberg's. Do you think knowing these stages would be more helpful to the person who is grieving or to that person's friends as they try to give comfort? Why?
5. How can a person prepare for a terminal illness in the family so that, when it hits, the family can, in the author's words, "take the high road"?
6. The author says, "When you go through a significant grief experience, you come out of it a different person." In what ways are you different? How can that be used to your advantage and to the advantage of God's kingdom?
7. Are you "on the wire" or just waiting? How can you get back on or be sure you stay "on the wire"?

[5]Anne Davison, 1974.

Dream Intruder #3

You're Fired!

There are many different terms for it:
- You got a "pink slip."
- They gave you the "boot."
- You were asked to "resign."
- You were "laid off."
- Your "contract wasn't renewed."
- There was a "plant closing."

But to you it all amounts to the same thing.

"YOU'RE FIRED!"

You go into work one morning and you're called in by your supervisor. She asks you for your keys and informs you that you have five minutes to gather your personal belongings and leave—and you're not to come back.

At the end of a day, your manager calls in the entire shift and says, "We will not be opening tomorrow. We're sorry." And when you go home that day, you may or may not have the wages you had coming to you.

You're called into your boss's office. He presents you with a letter that says, "I hereby resign my position, effective immediately," and your name is typed at the bottom of the letter. In his hand is a check for four weeks of severance pay. Your boss says, "I want you to sign this letter of resignation, and you can walk away with this check. Or we're going to let you go without any pay at all. Take your choice."

Whether you were asked to submit your resignation or were simply let go, it's the same thing emotionally. No job, no income, no reason to get up each day, no self-worth, and strained family relationships. You've met a dream intruder.

Lou Nell Bath writes, "In a very public and bitter dispute, I lost a highly visible job. Believe the surveys claiming that, next to the death of a loved one, losing a job is the most traumatic experience most of us endure. It was devastating.

"I retreated to a cabin on the lake where I wallowed in self-pity for months."[6]

Granger Westberg (*Good Grief*) tells of a man who was unexpectedly fired from a job he had held for twenty years: "I was so stunned by what they told me, I walked around as if I were in a trance. What they said just did not register. I heard the words, but they had not 'reached' me yet."

When you're fired, you go through very much the same grieving process that you experience when a loved one dies. First there is the initial shock and numbness. Then there is the anger and bitterness. And sooner or later, there is often the long, heavy depression that can so easily set in. This is especially intense for those who have held the same job for a long time.

Though being fired is never easy for anyone, it seems that men especially struggle with it because they derive so much of their self-worth and self-respect from their work, while women tend to gain their self-worth and self-respect from relationships and feeling loved. That's the reason the apostle Paul, in Ephesians 5, commanded husbands to *love*

[6]"What a Wonderful Web He Weaves," *The Lookout* (Standard Publishing, November 12, 1989), p. 2.

their wives and wives to *respect* their husbands. The basic emotional need of a woman is to be loved, and the basic emotional need of a man is to be respected.

If you've never lost a job, don't think it can't happen to you. At the very least you have a number of people around you who can use your help in getting through this dream intruder in their lives. They need your encouragement. God can use you in a significant way to help them dream some new dreams and get on a new track.

The book of James teaches us an important principle. James writes, "Consider it pure joy, my brothers, whenever you face trials of many kinds, because you know that the testing of your faith develops perseverance" (James 1:2, 3). The principle contained in those words is this: "Your attitude determines the outcome of the trial."

You can view trials in one of two ways. You can view trials as enemies or as allies. You can look at the dream intruder of losing your job as an enemy, the worst thing that ever happened to you. Or you can face it as an ally and say, "You know, this is an opportunity for me to develop some character. I'm discovering some rough edges in my life, and I'm going to work on them while I have the chance." Your attitude will determine the outcome.

Webster defines *crisis* as a "turning point." The Chinese term for *crisis* is made up of two symbols: one for despair, the other for opportunity. This dream intruder is very likely an opportunity for some positive things to happen in your life, but your attitude will determine whether capitalize on that opportunity or not. To get through this dream intruder, there are three questions that must be answered.

Why Was I Fired?

This question is crucial, because an honest answer will help you gain an important perspective on your situation. The reason you lost your job may have nothing to do with you, or it may have everything to do with you. So take some time, evaluate honestly, and ask, "Why was I fired?"

Maybe There Was a Misunderstanding

Maybe there was a difference of expectations. The expectations were never clearly spelled out, and your understanding of what was expected of you and your supervisor's expectations were totally different.

Maybe You Were Unsuited or Untrained for That Particular Task

Sometimes we accidentally get in a job that we're unprepared to handle. Either we don't have the education or it's not the area of our own giftedness and ability. In interviewing a job applicant, one employer said, "Young man, you are asking for some high wages for a man with no experience."

"Well, you see, sir," the applicant replied, "the work is a lot harder when you don't know anything about it."

A woman who had been very discouraged in her previous job in sales took a new job as an administrative assistant. She told me, "I love my new job. I figured out something. I've discoveredI'm not a point person. I'm a support person. That's where I excel. And I enjoy my work so much more now." Sometimes we just get in the wrong job.

Maybe You Were Unable to Concentrate on the Job Because of Other Distractions in Your Life

Sometimes we say, "When it rains it pours," and for good reason. Maybe there are problems at home, family problems, or other dream intruders. Maybe someone in your life is dealing with a terminal illness or a chemical dependency. Something is distracting you so that when you go to work, your head just isn't there. And now the dream intruders are pouring. Along with the big one that you were worrying so much about, now you've lost your job on top of it.

Some People Lose Their Jobs Because of Company Cutbacks

When people weren't buying your product, your position got phased out. Many U.S. automakers have down-sized their work forces by thousands of employees in order to stay competitive with the imports. The large hotels in Las Vegas annually make "seasonal adjustments" and cut back their work force during those times of year when the number of tourists goes down.

You Can Lose a Job by Being Slandered by a Fellow Employee

Maybe someone just didn't like you. Maybe he wanted your job. Maybe your work made his work look bad, so he spread some stories about you. He cast some suspicion on your work, your honesty, or your integrity. Have you heard of Conway's Law? It states, "In any organization there will always be one person who knows what's going on. This person must be fired." That could have been you.

Sometimes There's a Personality Clash With a Supervisor

Sometimes two people just can't gel together. You just never hit it off with your boss. From the day you arrived there was tension. Some people are just impossible to work with.

It's like the tongue-in-cheek new employee policy I came across recently. Supposedly developed by a supervisor, it states, "For sickness: no excuse. We no longer will accept your doctor's statement. If you are able to go to the doctor, you are able to come to work." Additionally, it said,

> Too much time is being spent in the rest room. In the future, we will go to the rest room in alphabetical order. For instance, those whose names begin with "A" will go from 8 A.M. to 8:05

A.M., "B" will go from 8:05 to 8:10 A.M., and so on. If you are unable to go at your time, you will need to wait until the day when your turn comes again.

Your own death will be accepted as an excuse for absence, but since we feel it is your duty to teach someone else your job, we'd like a two-week notice.

If your supervisor is anything like the one who wrote this policy, maybe he or she did you a favor by letting you go.

Now so far, all the reasons listed are outside of your control—at least primarily. However, just maybe you were at fault when you lost your job.

You May Have Been Fired for Good Reason

This is difficult to admit, and sometimes we can only admit it after some time has passed, because at first we are so angry. The human tendency is to place the blame on something or someone other than ourselves.

Maybe, as time went by, you got lazy. Proverbs 10:4 warns us, "Lazy hands make a man poor, but diligent hands bring wealth." We live in a day where our affluence has made many lazy. Someone said most young people today think Manual Labor is the president of Mexico.

Sometimes people steal from the company and lose their jobs. They get sloppy and quit paying attention to detail. They get obstinate and become uncooperative. Or they have to be told every little thing to do.

One big corporation had a young employee whose own evaluation of his worth to the company was far different from his supervisor's. The manager called him in one day and said, "Young man, did you know that you and the chairman of the board of this company have something in common?"

The young man puffed out his chest and said, "No. What is it, sir?"

The manager said, "You've both gone as far as you're going to go in this company!"

Employers are not looking for people with a lot of knowledge. They are looking for people who know how to apply knowledge, no matter what the field is.

Could you be honest with yourself and consider this possibility? Were you at fault when you lost your job?

When you are able to answer that question honestly, you are making your first major step toward getting through this dream intruder. If it was not your fault, you can appreciate your own abilities and start over. If it was your fault, you can begin to make some character adjustments or get some additional training or take some other necessary action to overcome whatever led to your dismissal.

How Can I Get Through This Depression?

Even with that honest analysis, it still doesn't change the fact that you lost your job. Often people slip into a time of depression, a feeling of helplessness. It comes because you face a situation that you feel is beyond your power to handle. The situation looks hopeless.

In 1 Kings 17 and 18, we encounter Elijah. He was a tremendous spokesman for God for three years to the nation of Israel. He performed all kinds of miracles. There had been a spiritual awakening in the land. In other words, he did his job well.

But when we get to 1 Kings 19, we discover there was one person who didn't like Elijah—Queen Jezebel. Just like in your workplace, problems can start with a personality clash with someone or a jealous co-worker. Jezebel hated Elijah, partly because he had so much influence.

After one particularly fantastic miracle that Elijah had performed (1 Kings 18:19-40), Jezebel got word that in the process Elijah had had the prophets of Baal executed. She then sent word to Elijah: "May the gods deal with me, be it ever so severely, if by this time tomorrow I do not make your life like that of one of them" (1 Kings 19:2). She was saying, "If I don't kill you in the next twenty-four hours, I'll kill myself."

Now here's fearless Elijah, who for three years has experienced remarkable success. But when one woman threatens him, he's frightened, thinks his job is over, gets depressed, runs out in the desert, sits down under a tree, and he prays, "I have had enough, Lord. Take my life. . . ." (1 Kings 19:4). Elijah was letting his negative thinking control his life.

Negative Mental Games

If you think negatively, you're going to get down. Elijah played five negative mental games that all of us play when we get depressed. First, *we focus on what we're feeling, not on the facts.* After Elijah's life had been threatened, he ran. Later he thought, "I'm such a coward. Why am I running? I'm a wimp." And because he "felt" like a failure, he assumed he "was" a failure. This is called emotional reasoning. The idea is, "If I feel it, it must be true."

All of us have a flop once in a while. When we do, we need to remember feelings are not facts; they are very unreliable. The fact that you've made a mistake does not mean that you're a total wipe out.

We label ourselves. Instead of saying, "I made a goof," we say, "I'm a total failure." Instead of saying, "I accidentally tripped," we say, "I'm a klutz." Instead of saying, "This wasn't the job for me," we say, "I can't do anything." We need to vent our feelings, but we need to be sure we remain honest with ourselves. The Bible doesn't tell us just to get in touch with our feelings, but to get in touch with the truth. It's the truth that sets us free. Focus on facts.

A second negative mental game we're good at playing when we're depressed is to *compare ourselves with other people.* Elijah said, "Lord, take my life. I'm not any better than my ancestors."

Most of us have fallen into the trap of thinking, "If I could just be like so-and-so, I'd be happy." When you start comparing yourself with other people, you're asking for trouble. The Bible says in 2 Corinthians 10:12 that such activity is unwise and harmful. The only person you can be is you. That's all God wants or expects.

When we compare ourselves with other people, we tend to compare our weaknesses with their strengths, forgetting that these people might have some weakness in areas in which we are strong.

Third, *we blame ourselves for things that aren't our fault.* Elijah said to God, "I have been very zealous for the Lord God Almighty. The Israelites have rejected your covenant, broken down your altars, and put your prophets to death with the sword" (1 Kings 19:10). In other words, "I've failed at my job. I really tried to reach them, but they're living the same way as before. I blew it." In his depression, Elijah blamed himself for failing to change the nation. But it wasn't his fault.

Sometimes we assume a responsibility that isn't ours. Seasonal layoffs and company cutbacks are not your fault. Maybe you're a salesperson, but nobody is buying your product. Maybe the problem is not the person, but the product.

Our fourth negative mental game is to *exaggerate the negative.* Elijah was having a pity party: "I am the only one left, and now they are trying to kill me too" (1 Kings 19:10). Elijah thought, "Everybody's against me," but the fact was everybody was not against him. Only one person— Jezebel—was against him.

When we get depressed, we exaggerate the negative, and everything looks bad.

- "I guess I'll never work again."
- "Who would ever want to hire somebody my age?"
- "No sense in going to work for anybody. I'll do them more damage than good."
- "I guess the world's just out to get me. There must be something about me that everybody hates."

Fifth, *we feel like we're all alone.* Elijah had the impression he was the only one left in all of Israel who was loyal

43

to God. Yet God reminded him that there were 7,000 faithful followers left in Israel (1 Kings 19:18).

Friend, remember you're not alone as you face this dream intruder. There is a church family who wants to help you. In every local Christ-exalting body, there are others who've gone through the same or very similar circumstances that you are going through. If you'll let them, they'll help you through this time.

Getting Over the Depression

Eventually Elijah worked through his depression. Along the way, we see some important tips for getting through the depression you go through when you're fired.

A good place to start is to take care of yourself physically. Elijah was physically exhausted, so he lay down under a tree and fell asleep (1 Kings 19:5). Then "an angel touched him and said, 'Get up and eat.' He looked around, and there by his head was a cake of bread baked over hot coals, and a jar of water. He ate and drank and then lay down again" (1 Kings 19:6). Then after some more rest the angel touched him again and he ate more (1 Kings 19:7, 8). The first thing God did to help Elijah was to get him physically restored.

If you've lost your job and are depressed, one of the best things you can do is to take care of yourself physically. How many times have you said, "I don't have time for exercise?" Well, now you do. Put it in your schedule. It can be anything from walks to jogging to calisthenics to tennis. You'll find it helps you mentally as well as physically. Maybe you need to watch your diet and start eating better.

Exercise, eating the right foods, and getting adequate rest all help overcome the negative feelings of depression. Often depression is the result of poor health. As health improves, the feelings of discouragement start to break up.

Along the way, *vent your frustrations.* God asked Elijah what he was doing in a cave (1 Kings 19:9), and Elijah just poured out to him all of his inner feelings. God allowed him to let off steam. Elijah was feeling fear, resentment, low self-esteem, and guilt. He was angry, lonely, and worried. When you get all those things together, you're asking for depression. So God just let him spill out the things that were eating him up inside.

You don't need to be afraid to lay your situation out to the Lord and to some friends. Often it's a cleansing, a catharsis, to get out all of those things that have been pushed down inside of you and are causing your depression.

Let God speak to you. When we're depressed, we need to hear from our Maker. God told Elijah to go out and stand on the mountain because he was about to pass by. Then a powerful wind tore the mountain apart and shattered the rocks, but the Lord wasn't in the wind. Then an earthquake came, but the Lord wasn't in the earthquake either. After the earthquake came a fire, but the Lord wasn't in the fire. But then, after the fire, came a gentle whisper, and Elijah put his cloak over his face (1 Kings 19:11-13). He knew it was the Lord. God spoke to him in a still small voice.

God usually speaks to us today in a still small voice. While you're out of work, listen to the still small voice of God. Develop your Bible study and prayer life. You've always said you didn't have time; now you do, so take advantage of it. Instead of a few minutes here and there, study for thirty minutes or an hour a day. Put it in your schedule and make it a part of your routine.

When we stop long enough and let our lives get quiet enough to hear the still small voice of God, there is so much we can learn. You might learn that in your last job, you had messed-up priorities. Maybe you were a workaholic. Maybe you were just the opposite. Maybe you learned God has a different plan for you.

A man told me apologetically one day he had quit his job. He had been working six and seven days a week, twelve to fifteen hours a day. He said, "I took some vacation time and decided it wasn't worth it. But you know, Gene, I feel like a quitter."

I said, "I'm so proud of you! You have discovered there are other things more important in life. You've discovered there are some priorities to be established. I think God will honor that."

I'm not sure that man would have come to this realization if he hadn't had a few weeks off to listen to the still small voice of God.

One of the best things to do when fighting depression is to turn outward. The Lord told Elijah, "Go back the way you came, and go to the Desert of Damascus. When you get there. . ." (1 Kings 19:15). The Lord gave Elijah a new job, a new career, a new focus. He gave him a task to do that would turn him outward instead of looking inward.

The quickest way to defeat depression is to quit sitting around in self-pity. Get your eyes off yourself and start looking at the needs of other people. After you lose a job, there's a tendency to withdraw. After all, it's embarrassing to admit that you don't have a job. A lot of people won't know what to say to you. But hold your head high and socialize. Continue to relate to people. Be concerned about them. Who knows? Maybe your involvement with others will help you find a job. Use some of your new spare time to volunteer somewhere. It really helps to turn outward.

One minister went through such a stage of depression that he couldn't even get up to speak to his congregation. It went on for months. He was practically non-functional. Do you know how he got through it? He started writing letters of appreciation to other people, thanking them for something. He wrote letter after letter, and after he had written five or six hundred, he started to come out of his depression! He focused on other people.

How Can I Cut the Strings With the Past and Move Forward?

How do you put being fired behind you once and for all? You need two things: a new beginning and a new motivation.

A New Beginning

Let God give you a new direction for your life. Maybe the reason you lost your job was not your fault, but then again, maybe it was. Maybe you blew it. Maybe you made some bad mistakes in your past. Whatever the reason, God can still give you a new purpose and a new direction. He's not through with you.

Did you blow it? Big deal! If you let him, God will pick you up and give you a new start. One mistake—or even a hundred—does not make you useless for life. Jesus Christ came to forgive us of our sins. When he forgives, he forgets. To stew over our past failures is deadly. It takes away our ability to hope.

Jesus Christ wants to lift you out of your depression. He can help you. He can change you. The apostle Paul didn't have a great past that he was proud of, but through the grace of Christ he said, "Forgetting what is behind and straining toward what is ahead, I press on..." (Philippians 3:13, 14).

The new beginning starts by establishing a personal relationship with Jesus Christ. You become what the Bible calls "born again." It's a whole new birth. This new beginning may not cure all of your depression, and you may not get a new job right away, but without Christ in your life you have no power to change.

Jesus came so "that you might have life and have it abundantly." Jesus Christ, the Son of God, wants to be a vital part of your life. If you give him control, he will help you.

As a Christian, you will find he gives you a new purpose and a new meaning in living. You need something greater to live for than just yourself. People who live for themselves are guaranteed to get depressed. You need something greater that draws you out of yourself. And that is a vital relationship with Christ.

Maybe this is your opportunity to find the career that excites you. Fulfillment has little to do with the salary you're making. Pray God would give you an opportunity to find something that really expresses who you are. Decide you're going to get up each morning and make something worthwhile of the day during this transition time. Don't let your life turn into a series of long naps or staring at the walls with the television on. Schedule projects, resumé writing, job searches, yard work, and anything else that is a part of your life. You've got an opportunity for a new beginning and a new vision.

I like the T-shirt one college student was wearing as he was seen riding his bicycle across campus. In big letters across the back were the words, "I'M GOING TO BE A DOCTOR." And on the back of his bicycle was a little sign that said, "I'M GOING TO BE A MERCEDES." That's a vision. And you can have it with a new beginning.

A New Motivation

In addition to a new beginning, Jesus wants to give you a new motivation. In his letter to the Colossians, Paul included a section on a Christian's work ethic. In that context, he wrote, "Whatever you do, work at it with all your heart, as working for the Lord, not for men" (Colossians 3:23). As a Christian, you have a new work ethic. You're not working for your boss, for your family's needs, or for yourself. You're working for the Lord. Your best work can be an expression of worship to him.

When you work as working for the Lord, you'll be an employee no organization or business can be without. One man who had experienced unemployment found himself at forty-five years of age without a job, and in the most financially demanding years for his family. No matter where he went, he got no encouragement. In desperation, he ran an ad listing his fascinating qualifications: "Money-back guarantee. If you choose to employ me, and after ninety days find I'm not as good as I say, you'll get back 75% of everything you paid me."

Could you run an ad like that? Christ can give you that new motivation. Let your life and work be an expression of gratitude for the grace he has extended your way.

Snowflakes are beautiful little crystals. They glitter like diamonds. Each one has six points, and they all are symmetrical. But did you know that those beautiful snowflakes come into existence because at the center of each one is a tiny bit of dust? The water vapor that turns into a snowflake always collects around a piece of dust. It's that little foreign intruder of dust that helps a snowflake form.

In the same way, the dream intruder of being fired can be the catalyst to something wonderful in your life. Maybe it's led you to seek the Lord for the first time in a long time. Maybe it's helped you to get a fresh perspective on what you want to do the rest of your life. Maybe Christ has given you a new beginning and new motivation.

God's in the business of doing some beautiful work through dream intruders. Being fired is no exception.

Questions for Discussion

1. Imagine your reaction if you were to report to work tomorrow and find you no longer had a job. What would be the hardest aspect of the situation to accept or deal with?
2. Look back at chapter 2 and find the stages of grief described by Elisabeth Kubler-Ross and Granger Westberg. How are many of these stages comparable to one's reaction to losing a job? How are they different?
3. How does one develop the character necessary to take a positive attitude in a crisis—an attitude that makes it an opportunity for growth instead of an excuse for despair?
4. List as many reasons as you can think of for losing a job. List them under two headings: "Not My Fault" and "At Least Partially My Fault." Suggest a proper response for each one.

5. Compare Elijah's situation in 1 Kings 19 with the loss—or potential loss—of a job. How does God's advice to Elijah help someone in that situation?
6. What are some negative lines of thinking commonly associated with losing a job? How can a person change negative thinking to positive thinking? What potential dangers are there in simplistically telling someone to have a positive attitude?
7. The author suggests venting one's frustration. What safeguards ought to be used when venting your frustration? Why?
8. Make a list of projects one could undertake to become outwardly focused instead of inwardly focused. Which of these could be done by an *employed* person as well as an unemployed one?
9. If you could find "the ideal job," one that is personally rewarding, pays well, and even enhances your ability to be a witness for the Lord, what would it be? What can you do right now—whether you currently have a job or not—to prepare to have that job? Make this your vision, and make a new beginning toward that vision.

Dream Intruder #4

Prodigal Children

For thousands of years, little screaming bundles of new life have been coming into this world. New parents can sometimes put us in a difficult position when their newborn baby is just days old and they say, "Isn't that just about the most beautiful baby you've ever seen?" It's uncomfortable because it's often not at all true, but who would dare say so? I've seen quite a few newborn babies in hospital maternity wards, and many of them are not all that attractive.

I have thirteen nieces and nephews. I love them all very much. They've all grown up to be pretty good-looking kids, but you never would have guessed it when they were born. My nephew Brian is a good-looking college student today, but when he was born, they had some complications and had to use forceps on his little head in the birthing process. As a result, he head was greatly enlarged, making him look like a little Martian or something. He had red marks all over his face. His eyes were swollen. His face was puffy. I think maybe this explains where we got the phrase, "a face only a mother could love."

Most parents will tell you that the sight of newborn babies was not all that attractive to them, until it was the sight of their own baby. Anybody else's wasn't such a big deal, but when they had their own baby—suddenly they held in their hands a little miracle. This tiny, precious bundle of joy is the most beautiful child in the world to them.

Exciting Dreams

We have an annual baby recognition and parent dedication Sunday at our church. You can just see the love in the eyes of those parents as they hold those little people in their arms and ask for God's help in their vital task of raising and shaping these little human lives. If you could ask those parents, "What do you think the future holds for your child?" I think you would hear some pretty exciting dreams.

When parents hold that little one in their hands, they dream they are holding onto greatness. What mom and dad don't dream that their child is going to grow up to be somebody very special? They dream that their children will do the things and become the things they never had the chance to. Parents dream their child will become the next Albert Einstein, the next Billy Graham, or the next Michael Jordan. They dream their child may grow up to find a cure for cancer or help bring about world peace.

A mother dreams about the day her daughter will become a mature young woman, and they will be able to sit down and have heart to heart mother/daughter chats by the fireplace. She wants to share with her daughter the deep truths she has learned in life. She dreams her daughter will open up and share her innermost feelings about life, love, and her future.

A father dreams that his little girl or little boy will one day carry on the family business or trade. He dreams of passing the baton, passing the torch, the mantle to the next generation. He dreams of the great hours together as he shares the wisdom and skills he has acquired through the school of hard knocks.

Parents dream their children are going to grow up with strong moral fiber and conviction, that they will be devoted to their families, hard working, and faithful. They expect that their children will be dependable, ideal fathers and mothers, and perfect mates.

And when parents look at their little blessing called a baby, it's just impossible to imagine this child could grow up and cause any kind of heartbreak, isn't it? But as Clarence Darrow said, "The first half of life is ruined by our parents and the second half by our children." I know that's a cynical gross overstatement, but many kids do grow up and break their parents' hearts.

Part of what makes the dream intruder of a prodigal child so crushing is all of those tremendously exciting dreams you had when you rocked the cradle. Reality started to set in a little bit when your child got in school and you realized he was just normal. He was a good student, but not an Albert Einstein. He was an O.K. athlete, but not a Michael Jordan. Maybe he was even a leader in the church youth group, but he's most likely not the next Billy Graham. In fact, you found out in some ways he was just an awful lot like you.

I don't know what the statistics are. It's more than what we'd like it to be, but it seems that most families have at least one child who ends up breaking the parents' heart one day. You always thought, "That won't be my child. Other people have prodigal children, but not me." Then it happens to you. Maybe it begins with a series of incidents. Or maybe it's one big jolt. Your child runs away. Your daughter is arrested. Your son is selling drugs. Your child who you thought was all grown up, mature, and now a family person of her own, suddenly leaves her husband and runs off to who knows where with another man. Your son informs you he is gay and wants nothing to do with you, your life, or your values. There is just no peace between you.

Some parents with prodigal children have no idea where their children will be spending the night tonight, who they'll be with, what they'll be doing. Maybe they're chemically dependent, controlled by alcohol addiction or crack addiction.

Heartbreaking Realities

Parents who've experienced the heartbreak of a prodigal child could give 1001 different scenarios. The dreams of the heart-to-heart talks by the fireplace and passing on the family trade or business have all but faded away.

The feelings that a parent of a prodigal child has are almost indescribable. A chair sits empty at the dinner table. Family activities are subdued. Your child's name is rarely, if ever, mentioned. It's almost as if someone has died. Your child has rejected his home, family values, faith, and ethics in search of a magical word he calls "freedom." You have prayed and prayed and prayed for him until you are blue in the face. You keep praying that somehow God will miraculously bring him to his senses. You keep praying for some kind of divine deliverance, but time just keeps passing by and there's still no miracle.

The emotional pressure begins to be felt in other family relationships. It's like the message on a plaque one mother had hanging in her kitchen. It said, "When mama ain't happy, ain't nobody happy!"

The parable of the prodigal son in Luke 15 is the story of a son who took his inheritance early; ran away to a foreign land; squandered everything he had; hit rock bottom and ended up working in a pig pen; and finally returned home, bankrupt, on his knees, and his father restored him. You dream of your prodigal child's doing the same thing, but you know this parable Jesus told is only a story. There are no guarantees that your situation is going to change.

You replay in your mind every day of your child's life, from the day he was born. You analyze every experience, every situation, every activity, every date. You just keep asking yourself, "Why did it happen? Where did we go wrong?" You are tortured with the thought it's your fault.

So let's just analyze some of the possible negative influences a parent might have on his or her child.

Possibly You Were an Overindulgent Parent

A lot of parents today pour out material goods on their children, thinking it's an expression of love. In reality, it may be doing serious damage. They give children closets full of clothes, half of which they don't wear, and all kinds of toys and gadgets they take for granted. The children have tricycles before they can walk, ten-speed bikes before they can ride, and cars as soon as they turn sixteen. Such children never learn what it is to have to work for something. They never know what it is to want something so very badly but have to wait for it—and then to rejoice when it comes. They never know what it is to desire something and not get it.

Proverbs 21:17 says, "He who loves pleasure will become poor." Children who have had all the pleasures they ever wanted are not prepared for the harsh realities of life. They get depressed when they discover later in life that they aren't the center of attention any more. They become extremely hostile toward anyone who refuses them anything. They become disillusioned in marriage when their partners don't meet their every desire the way their parents did.

Maybe You Were a Negligent Parent

As you look back, maybe you can see some negligence. We live in the day of the "latch-key" child. Mom and Dad are both busy working. Kids come home from school and baby-sit themselves. After work, Mom and Dad stop at the gym to work out while the kids start dinner. In the evening, the folks have a meeting, or they are worn out and snooze in front of the television set. The kids are left to do their homework by themselves, and their questions go unanswered. Many neglected children are not from poverty-stricken families, but from families whose parents care more about their own needs than about their kids.

In the Old Testament books of 1 and 2 Samuel there is recorded the story of King David and his son Absalom. David was a great public success. The story of his thrilling career reads like the biography of Lee Iacocca. He became king, not by his birthright, but by his sheer ability. He rose up through military ranks by killing the Philistine giant Goliath with one expertly aimed stone from a slingshot when he was just a boy. He had the genius of a poet. He was good looking, and everyone who came into contact with him was spellbound by his irresistibility. He was a warrior who won victory after victory, expanding the bounds of his nation. Financially, he was a great success—so much so that throughout Israel's history they looked back to David's day as the "Golden Age."

But while David was succeeding publicly, he was failing at home. He didn't give his son Absalom any time. He was too busy conquering territories, winning wars, cutting deals. Sure, he was out working hard and providing for his children the things he never had as a child, but he neglected giving them any time. James Dobson writes, "We're so concerned about giving children what we didn't have growing up that we neglect to give them what we did have."

Some Prodigal Children Are the Sons and Daughters of Prodigal Parents

Why should a young person obey his parents who tell him not to take drugs, when he sees Mom and Dad consuming large quantities of the drug of alcohol? How much stock does a child put in his parents' encouragement to avoid sexual promiscuity when Mom or Dad have an affair?

I read in the paper about a seventy-six-year-old husband and his sixty-two-year-old wife from Florida. They plotted with their son to kill their son's ex-wife in order to collect a $35,000 life insurance policy. But after the murder, they found out the policy had lapsed. Then the father, a retired automotive engineer, and his wife, who had worked for a major airline for twenty-three years, murdered the son to collect a $70,000 life insurance policy on him. With parents like that, is it any wonder kids become prodigals?

One of David's problems as a father the bad example he set. He disappointed Absalom so many times. When David had an affair with a beautiful young woman named Bathsheba, Absalom saw the cracks in his father's life. Absalom was so disappointed in his dad he took off to his grandfather's and left home for three years. Eventually when Absalom did come home, David gave him no more than a halfhearted welcome.

The disillusioned Absalom developed a rebellious spirit. He led a revolution against his father, the king. In the middle of that revolt, he temporarily took over Jerusalem, and out in public where people could see what was going on, Absalom slept with some of his father's wives. Now you tell me, where did Absalom get his example?

There are many other influences that we could list in trying to determine, "Why did this happen to my child?" We could list peer pressure, the state of our world, lack of discipline, abuse, and many others. But it is very important that you understand that everything we've just listed is an influence and not a cause. I have chosen my words carefully. Parents with a prodigal child, please read these words carefully: *Your actions influence your child's behavior. But that's all it is: **influence.***

Some of you parents are killing yourselves with guilt about what you did or didn't do that caused your children to make the poor choices they have made. Please understand something that you won't hear in too many other places, but it is clearly taught in Scripture. You are not the *cause* of your children's prodigal nature.

At a deep emotional and intellectual level, most parents today feel responsible for any failure their children have. Psychologists have said good parenting will produce good kids. And if things haven't gone as you planned, you think you weren't a good parent. Accordingly, the kids have learned to heap the blame on parents, adding to the guilt. Prodigal children cry, "They never showed me love. They never had time for me. I'm just a product of my environment. I turned to crime because we were so poor." One kid said, "We were so poor that we used to go to Kentucky Fried Chicken and lick off other people's fingers."

Parents, you don't cause your child's behavior. You may provide a positive or negative influence, but you are not the cause.

Biblical Insights

In order to see this even more clearly, let's get two biblical insights into your prodigal children.

Each Person Is Accountable for His Own Behavior Only

On the day of judgment, you will be accountable for you and you only. Your child will be accountable for himself and himself only. There's not going to be a chance for him to blame you, blame his environment, or blame the government. On the day of judgment, the blame game stops and every person will be accountable for himself.

Every person in life has the opportunity to make her own decisions. It's up to each of us to grow up and go on, even if we have been influenced by some bad circumstances.

You might have been a perfect parent. That's not likely, but there were some children once who had the Perfect

Parent, and those children still messed up their lives. Adam and Eve were the first children of God and the first prodigals in history. Think about all the positive influences they had. God placed them in a paradise, a land that he had created specifically for them. There was no death or decay. Adam and Eve had the benefit of the perfect environment, the perfect Parent, and the perfect instruction, yet they still rebelled and rejected their Father. There's nobody to blame for the prodigal nature of Adam and Eve but Adam and Eve. They made their own decision. They made their own choice. God was not to blame. Satan was not to blame. Adam and Eve had only themselves to blame. The only people eating the forbidden fruit were Adam and Eve.

After all is said and done, each person is responsible for his or her own actions. Children themselves must bear the brunt of their failure. Even though David had set a poor example for his son Absalom, Absalom was only one of a number of children, and not all of David's children became prodigals. Absalom chose his own negative course. However, some of the other children overcame the negative influences of their father and chose a positive course for their lives. If it had been totally David's fault, all of his kids would have turned out as prodigals, but every person makes his own choices and is alone responsible for his own actions.

There Are No Guarantees for Perfect Children

In the Old Testament, we find a father by the name of Samuel. He was a godly man. He was a man of prayer. He led an exemplary life. Yet his sons were prodigals. The only mistake that we know of that he made was to appoint his sons to succeed him as judges over Israel. They took bribes, made a travesty of justice, and took advantage of people. Imagine the grief, heartbreak, and embarrassment of Samuel. His example shows that even when a parent is godly, prayerful, and full of integrity, still there are no guarantees.

Some of you don't believe this. You are just so convinced that if you had been a better parent, your child would not have strayed. To back up your belief and to heap further guilt on yourself, you keep recalling Proverbs 22:6: "Train a child in the way he should go, and when he is old he will not turn from it." You say, "You see, I must not have trained my child in the right way, otherwise she wouldn't have wandered away. That verse promises me that if I train my child in the right way, she'll grow up and follow the right way. Don't you believe the promises of God, Gene?" I sure do, but Proverbs 22:6 is not a promise. It is a proverb.

There is a difference between an absolute promise and a general principle. The book of Proverbs is a collection of short statements that express general truths or principles that normally happen. So when Proverbs 22:6 says, "Train a child in the way he should go, and when he is old he will not turn from it," it is saying if you follow this advice, there is a good probability that your child will remain true to your instruction all his life or that he will one day return to God's teaching as he matures. But it's only a probability, not a promise.

There is no guaranteed path to perfect children. I know that doesn't take the hurt away when your children break your heart, but I hope it will help you stop blaming yourself and carrying guilt that is simply not yours to carry. I hope these two truths can free you from this emotional bondage.

Helpful Attitudes

I know you're wondering, "Well, how should I respond while my child is living as a prodigal? There's this big wall. I don't know what to do. We can't even talk anymore." I want to share four attitudes that I believe can be very helpful to parents with prodigal children.

Focus on the Person, Not the Behavior

Remember, the real problem with your child is not his sin, but the absence of Christ. His prodigal behavior is only a manifestation of that problem. Somebody said, "If you're controlled by the devil, you're going to live like the devil."

So focus on your child and not on what she does. Communicate that her chosen life-style does not affect your love for her. Don't let her behavior sever your ties as family. Let her know your love is unconditional. This doesn't mean you should financially support her in her chosen life-style and always bail her out of trouble, because she needs to experience the consequences of her own choices. But you need to focus on your love for her and not on your disappointment with her behavior.

Be Quick to Listen and Slow to Speak or Get Angry

This, of course, is the advice of James 1:19. Are you listening to your child? Are you hearing what has led him to take this path he has chosen? As you listen, you will know better how to talk to him. He already knows you are disappointed with his choices, so let him know you love him. He may think you're using your faith as a baseball bat, so let him know God loves him and that Jesus died for everybody. But listen, listen, listen to what he is saying.

Don't Argue About Behavior

There will be times your child will get defensive. "Oh Mom, Dad, you're so small minded. You're living in the stone age. Only people with hang-ups like you condemn people like me." Let her know you're not condemning. You love her and will always love her. There will be some things just better left unsaid, especially if you say it only with an intent to hurt her.

Remember, behavior is not going to change until a person's heart changes. There's no use arguing about the person's behavior, because people out of step with God are not going to act and walk as if they actually are in step with him.

Share Your Testimony About God's Grace in Jesus Christ

This is the ultimate goal. When the prodigal son returned home in Luke 15, the father celebrated and said, "My son was lost, but now he's found." Your goal is that your child who is spiritually lost be spiritually found.

If you wanted to talk to a friend or neighbor about your faith in Jesus Christ, would you set the stage with him by being short-tempered and complaining about how bad his yard looked? Of course not. Would you lecture him at great length or ignore his questions? Not a chance.

Yet some parents refuse to discuss any different points of view with their children and at the same time demand that they believe exactly what they tell them. They think they can dictate to their kids as adults. They think they can badger them into faith or nag them out of a sinful life-style.

Parents, maybe the greatest witness you can ever have with your kids is just to tell them, emotionally, how much Jesus Christ means to you. Have you ever told your child about how God's power and grace has worked in your life? They know you go to church. They know you pray. They know you read your Bible, but have you told them what Jesus means to you?

Possibly you realize that you can't help your child spiritually until you get right spiritually. When you do, you will be able to say with conviction to your son or daughter, "Honey, I'm afraid that I've never really told you that my faith is more than just going to church or being good. My faith in Christ is the most important part of my life. Someday I hope you'll be able to see that you need this relationship with him, too."

A positive witness tends to foster a spiritual thirst in your child as you demonstrate your own trust in the Lord. Again, there are no guarantees, but God uses a parent's positive witness time after time to bring home prodigal kids to him.

Are you a hurting parent? Then remember our heavenly Father has prodigal children, too. You probably can begin to understand better than anyone else just a little bit of the heartbreak God must feel over the billions of prodigal children in the world.

Jesus' parable about the prodigal son is really about how our heavenly Father deals with us, his children. The father of the prodigal son didn't just rejoice because his son had come home. If his son had come home with the same rebellious spirit he had when he left, there would have been no reason to rejoice. However, the prodigal son returned home bottomed out. He came seeking the fellowship of his father. He came respecting the authority of his father. And his father rejoiced.

That's what our heavenly Father waits for in all of us. He waits for us to bottom out and say, "Lord, I need your grace. Jesus died for me. I want to appropriate his sacrifice toward me. I want to make him my Lord."

We all need Jesus Christ. If you haven't already, why don't you seek his fellowship and accept him? Submit to his authority, confess your belief, and celebrate your decision by being baptized into Christ. The Father is waiting to welcome you home.

Questions for Discussion

1. If you are a parent, what are some of the dreams you first had for your child/children? If you are not a parent, what are some of the dreams your parents had for you? What has become of those dreams?

2. The author expresses the frustration of many parents when he says, "You have prayed and prayed and prayed . . . until you are blue in the face. . . . and still there's no miracle." How does a parent maintain faith in the face of so many seemingly unanswered prayers?

3. What kind of parental activities can contribute to a child's becoming prodigal? What can parents do about these things?

4. The author quotes James Dobson, "We're so concerned about giving children what we didn't have growing up that we neglect to give them what we did have." How much of "what we didn't have" is healthy for children? How can parents be sure to give "what we did have"?

5. Why is it significant to note that a parent's actions influence, but do not cause, a child's behavior? Where does Proverbs 22:6 fit in? Do you agree with the author that Proverbs 22:6 is not a "promise," but a general principle? Why or why not?

6. The author notes that everyone is accountable for his own behavior only. For whom is this fact more significant, the prodigal, who must face his own responsibility; or the parents, who may be blaming themselves for the prodigal's behavior? Why?

7. List the four suggestions for how to respond to a prodigal child that the author suggests under the heading "Helpful Attitudes" (pages 60-62). Which is hardest to do? Which do you think is most significant from the parent's perspective? Which do you think may be most significant from the prodigal's perspective? Why?

8. Is there ever a time to "shut the door" on a prodigal? Can the prodigal reach a point where the parent must say, "You are not welcome here until you repent"? Why or why not? If so, how does one determine when that point has been reached?

9. Can you think of any other ways a parent might respond to a prodigal child? List as many ideas as you can. Then go back and evaluate each one. How many helpful ideas can you come up with?

Dream Intruder #5

Bankruptcy

The terms "chapter 7" and "chapter 13" may sound like sections in a book to some people. To many others, the only book they bring to mind might be a Stephen King novel, for they've experienced the real-life horror of personal bankruptcy.

We have some big personal financial problems in our nation. Eighty percent of the people in the United States have more debts than assets. The Social Security Administration tells us only 2% of Americans reach age 65 financially independent. The rest depend on charity (30%); continued employment (23%); or relatives (45%).

One wife was exasperated with her husband, who refused to go look for work. She said, "I'm ashamed of the way we live. My mother pays our rent. My aunt buys our food. I'm ashamed we can't do better than that."

"You ought to be," said her husband. "You have two uncles who don't send a dime."

Unfortunately many Americans are dependent on others for financial survival. Eighty-five out of 100 Americans have less than $250 when they reach age 65.

The problem is greater than just a lack of assets. Additionally, we tend to accumulate debt today at an enormous rate. According to the federal reserve, Americans are carrying more than $600 billion in consumer debt, which doesn't even include home mortgages. That's twice as much as the level of consumer debt we carried in 1981. So it's no coincidence that personal bankruptcies have doubled in the last decade. For some, the accumulation has been so rampant that they see it as the only way out. In Nevada, where I live, fourteen out of every 1000 households have filed for bankruptcy.

Bankruptcy is the declaration that you are unable to meet assumed debts or obligations either partially or completely. Only those who have faced this dream intruder in their lives know how devastating bankruptcy really is. To the majority of people who file, it is emotionally devastating and often wrecks their health. It's a moral problem for many: they have given their word that the debt would be repaid, and now they cannot make good on that.

Even though bankruptcy has initially relieved some or all of their debts, they still have many other struggles. They live with the stigma of a bad credit rating for a number of years. It's virtually impossible to completely remove it. Bankruptcy brings a great deal of associated family stress, also. In more than 90% of divorces, people point to financial difficulties as a contributing factor.

Many who have experienced this dream intruder testify it was like a snowball that turned into an avalanche as they were sliding down a mountain. There was an accident, a health problem, an unforeseen mishap that brought tremendous financial pressures, eventually leading to bankruptcy. Now they have lost everything: their business, their home, their family, and their self-esteem. Their self-image is so poor right now, they feel like they don't only have bankrupt finances, but they have a bankrupt life!

If you are facing the dream intruder of bankruptcy right now, I hope in this chapter you will find hope for climbing out of this black hole. I can't guarantee you this will be a painless journey. But if you will approach this journey honestly, objectively, and non-defensively, you can emerge from this dream intruder a much better person.

Whether you've experienced personal bankruptcy or not, there are some important lessons in this chapter all of us can learn along the way. Let's consider three questions: Why did it happen? How could it have been avoided? What should you do after the fact?

Why Did It Happen?

Some people start to get themselves in trouble with something as seemingly harmless as *impulsive buying.* Proverbs 21:5 says, "The plans of the diligent lead to profit as surely as haste leads to poverty." What's that saying? It's saying, "Don't be impulsive. Plan well. Think ahead, because acting hastily will eventually lead you to poverty."

We see a bargain in the paper that says we can save 50%, and we think, "Fifty percent!!! That's just too good of a deal to pass by." Now, you don't really need it, but you are saving so much! The truth of the matter is, you could save 100% just by staying home!

The seemingly innocent desire to buy on impulse begins to create a dangerous trend in your life.

In another case, bankruptcy might have occurred because of *poor management.* If most people were asked why they continued to accumulate personal debts, they would respond by saying, "I don't make enough money. I need more money." However, the problem is usually not how much one makes, but how much a person spends. If I asked you, "Do you think you could live on $10 million for the rest of your life?" you would probably say yes. Texas millionaire and former governor John Connally had $10 million, but that wasn't enough. He and a partner borrowed hundreds of millions of dollars for some real estate deals. The deals went bad, and they lost everything. The world watched as most of his worldly possessions were sold at public auction. The television cameras zoomed in to record the tears in his eyes as he embraced his wife and watched as personal item after item was auctioned off to the highest bidder.

Many in my city could tell you the story of how a simple day or night out gambling became an addiction and ruined them. The deeper they got, the more they gambled, hoping they could get out. Gambling is a tough addiction to break. If you've got the addiction, you need help.

It's not how much you make, but how much you spend. Financial counselor Larry Burkett tells of meeting with a couple who said, "We don't make enough money. Our total income is only about $15,000 a year, and that's not enough to live on in this area." He gave them a budget form and had them write down everything they were spending. Sure enough, $15,000 was not enough. The next couple came in and said, "We only make about $25,000 a year, and that's not enough to live on in this area." They filled out a budget form on everything they were spending, and sure enough, $25,000 was not enough money. The third couple came in and said, "We're only making $75,000 a year, and that is not enough money to buy what we need." They filled out the same budget form, and sure enough, they didn't make enough money. Now if he could have given that first couple making $15,000 a year a $75,000 income, they would have left thinking they were the wealthiest couple in town. But most likely they would be back in that financial counselor's office within two years with the same problems they had when they only made $15,000. It's not how much you make, but how much you spend. These couples didn't have an income problem, they had a management problem.

Another reason many people find themselves in bankruptcy is their excessive *belief in the "buy now—pay later" philosophy.* When we get into debt, debt doesn't look like debt. It looks like a new car, a new home, a new boat, a new swimming pool, a wonderful two-week vacation, or the best Christmas you've had in years.

Current marketplace wisdom says to you, "Raise your standard of living by buying what you want now and paying for it while you enjoy it." But the reality is, you may be sentencing yourself to a lower standard of living in the future.

Today, the average American has seven credit cards and owes $3,000 on them. If you just charge $600 on credit cards at Christmas, and you intend to pay it off in minimum monthly payments, you will still be paying for this year's Christmas three years from now!

For many, the problem goes much deeper. We get unsolicited pre-approved credit applications in the mail regularly. I saved mine for about a year and a half once. At the end of seventeen months, I had been offered $260,000 worth of credit! Now, I can think of a lot of fun things to do with $260,000—and so can you. But the fun would be pretty short-lived when the interest payments started coming due. We have automatic overdraft protection on our checking account, so instead of overdrafts we have a debt and finance fees. We can buy furniture or cars and not have to make any payments for three months or until next year! But all the while, the interest is accumulating. Meanwhile, we get deeper and deeper and deeper in debt. Eventually we realize the truth of Proverbs 22:7, which says, "The borrower is servant to the lender."

You may wonder, "Does the Bible teach that it's wrong to borrow money?" The answer is no, the Bible does not *forbid* borrowing, but it does *discourage* it. In fact, every Biblical reference to borrowing money is negative. The Bible teaches that when you borrow money, you are making a promise to repay. Literally, borrowing is making a vow, and God wants us to keep our vows.

Don't be fooled by the "buy now—pay later" philosophy. Proverbs 27:12 says it well: "The naïve proceed and pay the penalty" (NASB).

Sometimes bankruptcy is necessary because of *circumstances beyond our control.* Someone told me his wife had filed for divorce, and just before the divorce was final, she went out and charged thousands and thousands and thousands of dollars worth of goods. She was planning to declare her own bankruptcy, but legally, he was responsible for half of those debts. The circumstances were out of his control. He had not created them, but he was responsible for them, and there was no other way out.

Sometimes there is an unforeseen turn in economic conditions. For some unexplained reason that couldn't have been forecast, the economic climate takes a sudden change. During the 1970s, farmland prices in the U.S. skyrocketed. Thousands of farmers borrowed against the equity in their family farms, but when land prices and crop prices dramatically fell at the same time, thousands of families lost everything. Many of these family farms had been in their families for generations.

Economic conditions can turn during a natural disaster—like a tornado, an earthquake, a flood. When the bottom dropped out of the Texas oil market in the 1980s, it wasn't just the oil producers who were affected, but almost every other industry in Texas suffered some kind of adverse effects.

Some people go bankrupt because they are swindled by dishonest people. Others are forced into bankruptcy when a medical emergency in their family runs up into the hundreds of thousands of dollars. For others, a lawsuit coupled with heavy legal bills were the beginning of their demise. It can happen so fast.

Sometimes circumstances beyond our control force a bankruptcy.

I want to touch on one other reason that bankruptcy might have happened. This will be unpopular, but I really believe the root of many, many bankruptcies can be traced back to *pride*. Proverbs 16:18 says, "Pride goes before destruction, a haughty spirit before a fall." Pride is reveling in the thought of your own superiority over others. One way we think we can demonstrate that superiority is through the accumulation of things.

We live in a society with so much affluence surrounding us, it's hard not to get caught up in the race. I live in Las Vegas, Nevada, a city so affluent that we have a $40 million man-made volcano, surrounded by waterfalls and pools, that smells like piña colada when it erupts.

When your neighbors are upgrading their landscaping, it's easy to say, "Well, we'll see who is going to win the landscaping contest in this neighborhood!" You go into debt just to stay ahead of your neighbors. Do you see how pride can lead to financial problems?

The Bible warns frequently against having an inflated view of ourselves. James 4:6 says, "God opposes the proud but gives grace to the humble." Proverbs 16:5 says, "The Lord detests all the proud of heart. Be sure of this: They will not go unpunished."

Let's be honest with ourselves. In a deep moment of truth, wouldn't you have to admit many of your purchases or many of your business dealings or many of the debts that you've accumulated have been out of pride? Wasn't it more out of hoping others would see what you were doing than out of the objective management of resources?

The first question a person who has gone through bankruptcy must answer is, "Why did it happen?"

Could I Have Avoided It?

Hindsight is always 20/20, and maybe you can see some things more clearly now that you couldn't see at the time. Even if you have never had to go through bankruptcy, you need to pay careful attention to this point. What you learn may save you a lot of grief.

When asked, "Could you have avoided bankruptcy?" some people could say, "Maybe—if I had known the signs of trouble." Others might answer, "Perhaps I could have avoided it if I had counted the cost." Still others will say, "Yes, I think I could have if I had just acted sooner."

Watch Out for the Signs of Trouble

One article said the following signs are marks that you are likely headed for trouble. "You are headed for trouble. . . .

. . . if you see your credit cards as an addition to your paycheck instead of an expense that actually reduces your take-home pay."

. . . if you are only paying minimum monthly amounts due; making no deposits in saving, or withdrawing from savings to pay credit-card bills."

. . . if you are postdating checks so payments won't bounce or if you are hurrying to the bank on payday to cover checks you've already written."

. . . if you are charging more each month than you are making in payments."

. . . if you are taking cash advances on one card to make payments on another."

. . . if you are taking a cash advance to pay for regular expenses like rent, groceries, or gas."

These are signs that you need to pay attention to. I know you may think you're okay because everybody else does it, too, but that's the reason bankruptcies are increasing at such a rapid rate. There are people saying to themselves right now, "If I had only known the signs. I saw all of those things and didn't do anything about them."

Most of us are guilty of two common mistakes. The first is a *consumptive life-style.* A consumptive life-style is simply spending more than you can afford. It is spending more than you should, given your other financial goals. Proverbs 21:20 says, "A foolish man devours all he has."

The second common mistake is the *lack of a budget.* If you don't have a budget, you will tend to buy impulsively. When women buy impulsively, they tend to buy things like shoes, coats, and dresses. But it's not just women. Men also buy impulsively, but they tend to buy things like boats, cars, and second homes!

Most of us hate the thought of a budget because we view it as constraining. However, a budget can be one of the most financially freeing things there is. It's like a road map that tells you when you are off course. Not having a map creates fear, frustration, and anxiety. The same can be true for living without a budget.

Maybe bankruptcy could have been avoided had you known some of the signs in advance.

Count the Cost

Jesus said in Luke 14:28, "Suppose one of you wants to build a tower. Will he not first sit down and estimate the cost to see if he has enough money to complete it?" That's pretty basic advice, isn't it? Jesus is simply cautioning us against getting in over our heads.

Analyze your situation. How much is enough? How big does your house really need to be? How much furniture is really essential? How expensive a car will it take to satisfy you?

Good money management begins with a money manager who counts the cost. How often have you said something like, "The first of the year we're going to get a new car. Next April we're going to put on that new patio and cover. Next year we're going to get that new television"? But when the time came, you didn't have the money. What happened? You didn't count the cost. You forgot about all the other kinds of things. School began and the kids had to have new clothes and supplies. There were various fees, expenses, and tuition. You went on vacation. You went on some spur-of-the-moment weekend ski trips. There were birthday and Christmas gifts to buy. There were ball games and piano lessons. You didn't count the cost, so when the time came, you didn't have the money.

Take Action Before It's Too Late

Some might say, "Maybe I could have avoided bankruptcy if I had acted sooner." It's not too late for many of you. Other than those with business or investment losses, the average family can be out of personal debt in just two years if they will take three steps.

The first action you need to take is this: *don't go any further in debt.* One of the simplest economic principles ever written is, "If you don't borrow money, you can't get into debt." The second simplest economic principle is, "If you don't borrow any more money, you can't get further into debt." If you want to get out of debt, if you're heading toward bankruptcy, you've got to reverse the process that got you there.

If you find you're overspending each month on your credit cards, destroy them and mail them back in little pieces. You will be reversing the debt process.

The second action you need to take is *make out a realistic budget and control spending.* Don't promise to pay more than you're able to, but write each of your creditors a letter. Show them your budget and how much money you have available. Give them a list of all the other creditors, and divide your money proportionately. If you're only able to pay half of what you originally promised, tell them the truth. Believe me, lenders don't want you to go bankrupt. All they want is their money. With few exceptions, most lenders will try to work things out with you as long as you are honest and running towards them and not away from them.

Action #3 is to *pay back what you've promised.* Pay your creditors what you've committed each month. If any additional money comes in, use at least half of it to pay on your debts. Work on your smallest debts first. Then, as they begin to disappear, take the money you had been paying on them and apply it on the larger debts. You will have a sense of real accomplishment as you see them drop one by one.

Except in the case of some unforeseen circumstances, most personal bankruptcies could have been avoided if people had known the signs, counted the cost, and acted sooner.

But there is one kind of bankruptcy none of us can avoid. In Matthew 5:3, Jesus referred to "the poor in spirit." The word Christ uses for *poor* means one who is reduced to begging and is dependent on others for support. It means you are incapable of helping yourself; you can do nothing to meet your own needs. In the Old Testament, the Hebrew word for *poor* came to mean one was so broke he had no other alternative but to trust God.

You say, "Well, I'm not that poor." But Jesus wasn't talking about just material possessions or finances. He referred to the "poor in *spirit*." He was talking about what's on the inside of a person. He was talking about being spiritually bankrupt—spiritually unable to meet assumed debts or obligations.

Our sins against a holy God have created a debt that we cannot repay. Romans 6:23 says, "For the wages of sin is death." Sin is violating the standards of a holy God. The debt has to be paid because God is just. You wouldn't think very much of a baseball umpire who said, "Okay, here are the rules," but then never called strikes or outs. What if he sat around and said, "I just love all the players so much, I couldn't call a strike or an out on them"? It's the umpire's "sense of justice" that makes him a good umpire.

God is just, and when we sin, we violate his character, and the debt must be paid. It must be paid through death: physical death and spiritual death forever in eternity.

We are all spiritually bankrupt. This is a bankruptcy all of us have experienced. The Bible says, "For all have sinned and fall short of the glory of God." We all know this is true. We're not so full of pride that we can't at least admit this one; are we?. If you think you've lived a perfect life, just ask your spouse, your kids, or your friends and get their input.

The only way we can get out of spiritual bankruptcy is if someone else helps us. So let's ask our third question.

What Should I Do After the Fact?

I want to answer this question by considering both kinds of bankruptcies—financial bankruptcy and spiritual bankruptcy.

Don't Deliberately Make Creditors Bite a Larger Bullet

This first suggestion is for those who are on the verge of bankruptcy. I have known people who were in the process of working with their attorneys on filing their papers, and they have gone out and financed a new car and charged all kinds of other items—knowing full well they were not going to pay the debt.

That is dishonest. Such a person is borrowing with no intention of repayment. That is the kind of person Psalm 37:21 is talking about: "The wicked borrow and do not repay." When Christians do something like that, they hurt their testimony and the testimony of the church. They are a black eye in the kingdom of God.

Proverbs 22:1 says, "A good name is more desirable than great riches." I would encourage you to keep your commitments as much as is humanly possible, and never take on a debt that you know you can't repay. Stephen Brown says he believes for every non-Christian that goes bankrupt, there is a Christian that goes bankrupt so the world can see the difference. Christians need to show a difference.

I know some people who do the same thing spiritually when they're about to become a Christian. They reason, "Well, my life is going to take some changes, so I think I'll just deliberately go out and accumulate some more sin debts and have a little more fun before I make my decision." The problem is, that mind-set usually leads to further spiritual deception, and they never end up following Christ and receiving forgiveness of their sins. They were so close, but now they may never find their way back to the Lord.

If you're about to declare bankruptcy, don't deliberately make your debtors bite a larger bullet.

Make Restitution

Even after you've declared bankruptcy, I want to suggest, even now, make restitution wherever possible. The court may even relieve you from certain debts, but—as a sign of your integrity, and especially if you're a Christian, as a witness—make restitution.

I was impressed by one young man who claimed bankruptcy, but now, several years later, has gone back and tried to make restitution wherever possible. He told me, "Some of the businesses wouldn't take my money, saying the books were closed." I thought, "What a witness it must have been to see that kind of integrity."

When Zacchaeus, the dishonest tax collector, became a follower of Jesus Christ, he committed himself to repay four times the amount he had cheated from anybody.

Realign Your Priorities

If you have gone through bankruptcy, take some time to reflect on the direction and values of your life, and then *take appropriate action*. I know this has been an extremely painful time in your life, but it would be a great waste to go through all of this pain and not do some reflecting, and not learn from some of these experiences.

I hope you have learned something about the value of money. Somebody wrote:

Money will buy a house, but not a home.
Money will buy medicine, but not health.
Money will buy books, but not brains.
Money will buy glasses, but not vision.
Money will buy loyalty, but not love.
Money will buy a crucifix, but not a Savior.

Mike Singletary, the Chicago Bears' all-pro linebacker, said in the *Chicago Tribune:*

I never look at anything as mine. The talent I have, the house I have, the wife, the children, the friends I have. . . . they are not mine. I am just a steward of them. The Lord gave them and He can take them away. It is up to me to do the very best I can in showing God I appreciate it. Those things are very precious to me, but they are not my life. I'm never fearful of losing what I have because it is not mine to begin with.

Those are some priorities you don't see very often today. The only thing we can't lose is God. He is the same yesterday, today, and forever.

You say, "Well, how do I start getting my priorities straight?" You become "poor in spirit," as Jesus said. He said, "Blessed are the poor in spirit." The reason they are blessed, he says, is that "theirs is the kingdom of God." When you recognize your spiritual bankruptcy, you will know there is no other way out of this hole than for God to lift you out. And God can, because his Son Jesus Christ went to the cross and paid your debt of sin. He paid the wages of sin, which is death. Through the shedding of his blood, you can have forgiveness of your sin debts, but you have to appropriate it.

Bankruptcy can seem like the end of the world. You might be tempted to give up. But if you realign some priorities and the direction of your life, it might be the beginning of something better.

George Frederick Handel was paralyzed on one side. He was bankrupt, and his creditors were threatening him with imprisonment. For a brief time, he was tempted to give up. But he rebounded, and this broken, poverty-stricken man wrote his greatest piece of music, "The Hallelujah Chorus."

Lloyd Ogilvie has a friend named Ted who is a successful Chicago businessman. On Ted's desk is a plaque engraved with the words, "There's hope for you!" Lloyd asked him the story behind the plaque. Ted told him about an excruciating failure he'd gone through in the business world years before. He lost everything. At what he called the "bottom below bottom," Ted was forced to face his economic plight and his spiritual emptiness. Some Christian businessmen who met over lunch each Thursday in the Chicago Loop took him under their wing. One of the men always ended his conversation with Ted with the parting line, "Ted, there's hope for you!" Eventually, Ted began to believe it, and one day he committed his life to Christ. Ted says, "I was never a very hopeful person before meeting Christ. It's been nonstop hope ever since. I keep that plaque to remind me where I was and that I'm where I am today because of the Lord."[7]

Friend, there's hope for you, too. Bankruptcy is humbling, but sometimes we have to hit bottom before we look up and realize our need for the Lord.

When I was in high school, we used to sing a song in our church youth group that went like this:

> He paid a debt He did not owe.
> I owed a debt I could not pay.
> I needed someone to wash my sins away.
> And now I sing a brand new song:
> "Amazing grace," all day long
> Christ Jesus paid a debt that I could never pay.[8]

Questions for Discussion

1. According to the author, of Americans reaching the age of 65, only 2% are financially independent; 30% depend on charity; 23% depend on continued employment; and 45% are dependent on relatives. In which group do you expect to be when you reach 65 (or, in which group are you)? What do you plan to do about it?

[7]Lloyd Ogilvie, *A Future and a Hope* (Dallas: Word, 1988) pp. 104, 105.

[8]©1976, Gary McSpadden. Soro Publishing Co., Fourth Day Publishing, Dallas, TX.

2. The author lists five causes of bankruptcy: impulsive buying, poor management, belief in the "buy now—pay later" philosophy, circumstances beyond one's control, and pride. Which do you think is the major cause? Why? What can the church or concerned friends do to help people avoid bankruptcy?
3. What trouble signs does the author warn us to watch out for to avoid bankruptcy? What should a person do if he sees these signs in his life?
4. The author says, "Most of us are guilty of two common mistakes. The first is a *consumptive life-style.* . . . The second common mistake is the *lack of a budget.*" Are these concerns only for those who are headed for bankruptcy, or are these "mistakes" everyone should avoid? Why?
5. What does it mean to "count the cost" in terms of one's finances? How does a person do this?
6. The author says we need to "take action before it's too late." What action should you take to put a hedge between you and bankruptcy?
   ❏ Don't go any further in debt.
   ❏ Cut up your credit cards.
   ❏ Make out a realistic budget.
   ❏ Control spending.
   ❏ Work out a repayment plan with your creditors.
   ❏ Pay back what you have promised.
7. How is the situation of the one who has not accepted Jesus as Lord and Savior like the situation of one who is facing financial ruin? How might the similarities help us in dealing with either type of person?
8. The author suggests that the person who has declared bankruptcy and been declared legally free from his debts ought still to make restitution. Do you agree? Why or why not?
9. How can the attitude of Mike Singletary, "What I have is not mine, but God's," help a person avoid both financial and spiritual bankruptcy? Can you honestly say you live by the same standard? Why or why not?

Dream Intruder #6

Divorce

I'll never forget my first Christmas after the divorce. Does anyone? After our candlelight Christmas Eve services at the church, I intended to grab something to eat at a drive-thru, take it home, do some laundry, and pack for an early-morning flight back to the Midwest the next day to celebrate Christmas with my family. I got away from the church about 9:30 P.M., and I was starving. An early afternoon sandwich was all that had got me through the day.

I started driving around on this unusually cold and windy night, and absolutely nothing was open. Every fast-food restaurant was closed and the lights were out. I thought, "I'll get something in the deli at Smith's Supermarket. They're open twenty-four hours a day." But Smith's was closed. I've never seen Las Vegas (the city that never sleeps) so quiet. Nobody was on the street. It was like a ghost town. As I drove, I began to imagine that everybody was at home celebrating Christmas Eve with his family—except me.

By this time I was starting to get depressed. I was hungry. I was alone. It was Christmas Eve. I began to remember that Christmas Eve was always the time my family celebrated Christmas. But there was absolutely nothing to eat at my house, so I was determined to find something.

Finally, I headed out to a country-western themed casino that has four restaurants called Sam's Town. To my surprise, the place was hopping. I walked into their 50s-style diner and sat down alone at a table for four and ordered dinner. It was like a bad dream. I sat there eating the "blue plate special" thinking, "I can't believe it. I just spoke for over 2200 people, and here I am at Sam's Town on Christmas Eve eating meat loaf and mashed potatoes and gravy alone." Just when I thought it couldn't get any worse, someone put a quarter in the juke box and Elvis began singing in my ear, "Are you lonesome tonight?" I just started laughing to myself—maybe to keep from crying.

For a few moments that night, I had some of the loneliest feelings of my life. As I walked through the casino on my way out, I looked at all the people playing the slot machines and table games on Christmas Eve. I thought, "They don't have anywhere to go, either. They don't have anyone to be with tonight, either. Maybe this is their first or thirty-first Christmas since their divorce."

Divorce is ugly. The once "Ken and Barbie" romance is now a "Kramer vs. Kramer" war of the roses. It happens every day, all around us. *U.S. News And World Report* said marriages are being dissolved at the rate of one every twenty-seven seconds! And no one is immune. It affects all age groups. One fourth of the marriages of people in their early fifties will end in divorce. A fifth of all divorces involve people over forty who have been married longer than twenty-five years.

This chapter was hard to write. I read so much material. I thought. I contemplated. The more I worked, the more depressed I got. Divorce turns married couples into courtroom opponents. It removes children from parents. It separates brothers from sisters. Many experts say divorce is harder to recover from than the death of a spouse because it's not final. The other party lives on. Your lives, though no longer joined by marriage, are joined by memories, families, children, and finances. And the scars last a lifetime.

Struggles Faced by the Divorced

Even those who assumed divorce would be the road back to freedom and the answer to all their woes find the struggle of surviving divorce much greater than they ever imagined.

Divorce Is Painful

I thought losing my dad to a heart attack when I was just fourteen was the greatest pain I would ever know. But nothing I had known prepared me for the agony of divorce. The pain defies description. Divorced people everywhere are complaining about their plight on call-in radio programs, in counselors' offices, and on *Oprah* and *Donahue.*

Almost everyone experiencing divorce undergoes a "black" period when doubts, fears, anger, hostility, and vengefulness gnaw at her. She has fantasies about murdering the ex-spouse or the other woman. Even thoughts of suicide occur as she tries to resolve the difficulties in her mind.

Everyone who's been there will tell you there is a two-year crazy time that starts at the initial separation. Emotionally, the person is like a roller coaster—going from great feelings of hate and hostility toward those who've hurt him one moment, and then love and understanding the next because he knows hurting people hurt people.

Rash behavior like spending sprees, heavy alcohol or drug use, or a sex binge is common. A series of romantic affairs may occur in a mad rush to prove to oneself and to others that the person is of value to someone. But all this just brings even more pain.

If you're a man, you can't cry about it, can you? You've got to go to work and tell the other guys how relieved you are to be free. Inside, you cry, but you can't ever let it show. Yet it hurts. Losing hurts, no matter what anybody says.

It is painful to let go of the many things that were a part of the marriage experience. There are so many changes. One person described it as a "catapult from a four bedroom house in suburbia to an apartment in exile." You are confused, disoriented, frustrated, insecure, and uncertain.

Loneliness

Then, of course, there is the loneliness. Often they say to themselves, "If divorce is so great, why am I so lonely? Why am I so miserable?" The big vacuum inside longs for the ex-spouse; for children; for old friends; for former in-laws and family.

This loneliness leads some to make the mistake of jumping right into another marriage. We live in a world of "microwave" relationships. The moment one relationship ends, we jump right into another. People are trying to fix you up with their friends or cousins all the time. Dr. Paul Meier (*You Can Avoid Divorce*, Baker, 1978) says, when couples run away from their problems by divorcing and remarrying right away, "then there are four miserable people instead of just two.... Why spread misery?"

A man might go out and marry the woman with whom he has been having an affair. But if the problems in his marriage that led to the affair were never dealt with, he will just carry the same problems with him into the next marriage. While thirty-nine percent of first marriages end in divorce, sixty percent of second marriages fail. The problems just never get dealt with.

Financial Problems

A third struggle of divorce is finances. This is most often acute for women. With the arrival of no-fault divorce more than twenty years ago, many judges interpreted "no fault" to mean "no responsibility." Women must go right to work, and it's assumed they will become independent and self-supporting. Research shows, however, that while husbands experience a 42% rise in standard of living after divorce, women and children experience a 73% decline. Unfortunately, many of these women are becoming the nation's new poor. Only one third of the fathers pay their court-ordered child support; another third pay something some of the time; but the last third don't pay a single dime!

Scarred Children

Another struggle faced by the divorced is the effects on the children. A ninety-three-year-old man and his ninety-two-year-old wife had been married over seventy years when they came before a judge seeking a divorce. The judge asked them, "Why did you wait so long?" They said, "We wanted to wait till the children died."

The truth of the matter is no matter how old your kids are, it leaves a lifetime impact on them. Judith Wallerstein, co-author of *Second Chances: Men, Women, and Children a Decade After Divorce*, says:

> We've underestimated enormously the long term effect of divorce on children, and we need to address this economically and psychologically and provide much more understanding and help than we've been willing to.[9]

If kids have a tonsillectomy, their parents spend hours trying to help them understand, explaining, comforting. But in the midst of a divorce, parents often say nothing to the kids. They say, "Oh, kids are resilient. They'll bounce back." Nicholas Zill informed a senate sub-committee in 1983 that only one in five children maintains a good relationship with both parents after a divorce. Often, the home is the first

[9]Cited in *USA Today* (February 27, 1990), p. 9A.

thing to be sold after a divorce. Then the kids face the trauma of being separated from one or both parents, from their neighborhood, and probably from their school.

Many non-custodial fathers gradually disengage from their children after divorce. They don't exercise their visitation rights and don't see them. In a national sample, it was discovered that only one child in six saw his father at least once a week. Fifty-two percent of the children had had no contact whatsoever with their fathers in the last year.

There are many reasons divorce is damaging to children. It signals the collapse of the family structure, and the child feels alone and very frightened. Parents are preoccupied with their own emotions during the critical months or years of the divorce and have a diminished capacity to parent. There are conflicts of loyalty. Children wonder whose side they should take. They feel pulled in both directions. Uncertainty about the future causes insecurity. Toddlers often regress to an earlier stage of development. Young children tend to take responsibility themselves for the marriage breakup. Older children experience a lot of anger.

Acceptance

Then the divorced often struggle with acceptance. Your friendships have changed. The couples and families you used to socialize with are still your friends and you know they love you, but it's not the same any more. At times, you feel like a fifth wheel, and you wish you hadn't joined them for an evening out. But then other times, when you hear they did things with other couples or went to dinner or went camping, you're hurt that you weren't invited. You say to yourself, "I guess they just don't have room for me any more."

There are times when family members make you feel like a second-class citizen. "Well, you know, this is the first time this has happened in our family." An aunt or uncle makes the little dig, "Well, we've had our problems, too, but we always stuck it out and worked through them." Inside you burn with anger, seething with the thought, "If they only knew what I've been through. I shouldn't have to take this."

And then millions of Americans who have been at this low point in their lives decided that it was time they got their lives together spiritually. They reasoned, "Maybe God can help me. Maybe God will accept me. Somewhere in the back of my mind, I remember someone telling me that he is a specialist in putting together broken lives." So they went to a church, but instead of acceptance, they found judgment; instead of encouragement, they found rebukes; instead of being included, they were ostracized. A woman leaves saying, "I don't understand. I didn't want this divorce. I did everything I could to prevent it, to fight it, to keep it together. I was faithful, but he went through with it. And when I turned to the church for help, they said, 'Sorry, we don't have room for you here.'"

Don Baker tells of preaching a sermon on the amazing grace and forgiving love of a God, who could use a murderer like Moses as a great leader. When he got back to his office, there was an anonymous note on his desk that said, "It's a good thing Moses was only a murderer. If he'd been divorced, he would never have been asked to serve the Lord." Many divorced people want the grace of God, they want to know how God would have them move on in their lives, but so many churches keep them at an arm's length, and they're left hurting, confused, in need of a touch from God.

While churches have correctly stood for the sanctity of marriage, many have forgotten to balance their stand with the spirit of Christ, who specialized in accepting people nobody else would.

Guilt

Some divorced people wrestle with guilt for a long time: "What could I have done differently? Why didn't I make it work? I really failed. Look at all the damage my actions have done."

If you're struggling with guilt, the first thing you need to do is determine whether this is deserved or undeserved guilt. Many times people did everything they could do. They over-extended themselves to make the relationship work. Just as there are no guarantees good parents will raise good kids, there are no guarantees good spouses will have good marriages. Even though you weren't perfect, did you keep trying? Were you willing to hang in there and give it your best shot? If that's you, you're carrying undeserved guilt.

But then others of you are carrying deserved guilt. Some of you look back and say, "I was a real jerk. All I could think of was myself. My marriage fell apart because of my selfishness. I had an affair. I got out of step in my walk with the Lord. I shirked my responsibilities. I've not been fair to my children." Guilt like that can eat at you the rest of your life unless you deal with it.

I only know one way to deal effectively with guilt, and that is to place it on the shoulders of Jesus Christ, who died on the cross for our sins. Let the sacrifice of his blood atone for your sin. We can try to live a good life from here on out, but the guilt still has to be paid for. If you don't let Jesus carry the punishment, you'll carry it the rest of your life.

Move Toward the Cross

If you are carrying a load of guilt, you are in one of two positions: either you are a person who has never become a Christian in the sense of being born again from the inside by the Spirit of God; or you are a Christian who is in a position of disobedience. Either way, you need to do the same thing: *Wherever you are, move toward the cross.* If you've never been born again by the water and the Spirit, Jesus Christ wants to give you a completely new beginning.

Try to visualize him dying on the cross. Visualize placing every sin you've ever committed on his shoulders. Picture him carrying the guilt you're carrying. Friend, that's what he did on the cross for you. If you want to activate his forgiveness and salvation in your life, there are three things you need to do. *First, you must believe this message about Jesus,* which means you really trust him. *Second, you must turn from your sin.* The Bible calls this repentance. It means you start walking down a new path in your life. *Third, you must respond to Christ.* You respond by confessing the name of Christ and being baptized into Christ, which also symbolizes that the old you is dying and the new you is rising from the dead—free from sin, free from guilt, saved by grace.

If you are in Christ and you've been temporarily disobedient, you need to know there is a great cure for guilt. First John 1:9 says, "If we confess our sins, he is faithful and just and will forgive us our sins and purify us from all unrighteousness." The only requirement is that the confession must be sincere. You need to mean it and strive not to be disobedient any more. Just say, "God, I was wrong, and you were right. I've messed up, and I'm sorry. Will you forgive me and set me on the right track?"

Listen friend, God will cleanse the Christian believer right then and there—100%!

Wherever you are, move toward the cross. Once you're moving in the right direction you will be able to start working through the struggle of divorce.

God's Perspective on Marriage and Divorce

Once you're moving toward the cross, God's perspective on marriage and divorce becomes of paramount importance to you. We could write volumes in an exhaustive study of this subject, but let me try to sum up God's perspective on marriage and divorce with three truths.

First, God Sees Marriage as a Lifelong Commitment

Jesus said, "What God has joined together, let man not separate" (Matthew 19:6). He was literally saying people are not to divorce. Marriage is a permanent relationship unlike any other relationship. It is joined together by God.

That means, if you're considering a divorce, you need to back up and do everything you can to prevent it because God sees it as a lifelong commitment. That means, if you're married, you need to make a commitment to stay married.

On that dreadful night when my wife announced she was leaving because she was in love with another man with whom she had been having an affair for six months, I was devastated. But I had married her for better or for worse, so as far as I had anything to say about it, I was determined to keep my lifelong commitment. I knew reconciliation would be difficult, but I was determined to hang in there.

In most cases, divorce creates more problems than it solves. Diane Medved, marriage counselor, psychologist, and author of *The Case Against Divorce* (©1989, D.I. Fine), says:

> I've helped plenty of struggling couples through separation and "liberation." I originally thought that staying together in turmoil was more traumatic than making the break, that striking down taboos about divorce was part of modern enlightenment.
>
> I was wrong....Treating divorce as "morally neutral"—an option no better or worse than staying married—was irreparably damaging to the very people I wanted to help.
>
> Often in tears, the divorced people I talked with described fantasies of an ex-spouse returning or confessed guilt over abandoning a devoted mate....I'd ask, "Looking back, do you think you could have made it work?" ...Each side would conclude: "Knowing what I know now, yes, we could have made it work."
>
> ...Divorce may be the only recourse in cases of drug or alcohol addiction, physical abuse, severe emotional cruelty or permanent abandonment. But on balance, people could spare

themselves enormous suffering if they scotched their permissive acceptance of divorce and viewed marriage as a lifelong commitment not to be entered into—or wriggled out of—lightly.[10]

This is why God wants marriage to be a lifelong commitment. He knows what is best. He isn't trying to be hard on us. He wants us to have the best possible life. I've never had anybody say to me, "Divorce solved my problems."

Many of you may be tempted to "give up" because of the shock, hurt, rejection, emotional confusion, bitterness, and the pressure from others telling you to give up. But I want to tell you something you won't hear very often. Contrary to what a lot of people think, sometimes one person *can* save a marriage. Marriage counselor Ann Kristen Carrol says,

> If you think there's no hope because you are the only one in your relationship who wants or cares enough to try to save your marriage, you're wrong. In my experience most torn marriages are brought new life, new vitality, by the interest, basically of only one party.[11]

If you give up, there's no chance of it succeeding. But if you'll hang in there, believing God's grace is sufficient to help you handle the continual hurt, God's grace is sufficient to remake you into a better mate. God's grace is sufficient to sustain you when you are rejected.

This advice runs counter to everything the world will teach you. It runs counter to what some in the church will advise you—as they advised me. After you've been hurt by someone, giving him another chance goes against your human nature. But if we want to turn toward the cross, this is not the time to be arrogant or prideful. This is no time to

[10]Excerpted with permission from "The Trouble With Divorce," by Diane Medved, *Reader's Digest*, May, 1989, pp. 96-99. Used by permission of Donald I. Fine Publishers, New York.

[11]From *The Brick of Divorce* (New York: Doubleday, 1978), p. 19.

say, "Well, after what he's done to me, he's going to have to get on his knees and beg if he wants to come back now!" You can't exalt yourself saying, "Well, I'm not the one to blame here." You've got to humble yourself and patiently wait for God to do his work on the inside of your mate's life because, after all, marriage is a lifelong commitment.

Though He Hates Divorce, God Allows it in Certain Circumstances

God said in Malachi 2:16, "I hate divorce." Some people have read that and concluded, "This is a harsh God who doesn't understand what I'm going through," but God understands divorce very well. Do you know why? He himself is divorced. In Jeremiah 3:8, God says, "I gave faithless Israel her certificate of divorce and sent her away because of all her adulteries." God had a covenant relationship with Israel, but Israel didn't keep the covenant. God didn't want a divorce any more than many of you wanted a divorce, but it happened. So God knows all about the hurt and heartache of divorce. He understands what it means to be divorced. He knows what it is to be an innocent party on the short end of the stick. He knows failure in marriage does not make you a failure in life. He knows how to move forward after an unwanted divorce occurs.

You ask, "Well, when is divorce allowed?" Jesus taught divorce was allowed in the case of sexual unfaithfulness (Matthew 5:31, 32). Additionally, Paul taught if a Christian mate is left by an unbelieving mate, the Christian "is not bound" in such circumstances (1 Corinthians 7:15).

However, just because divorce is *allowed*, that doesn't mean it's *required*. God has worked in the midst of both of these situations many, many times and built stronger marriages. I've had many people tell me their marriages went through episodes of adultery, but they moved toward the cross. If I've heard this once, I've heard it a hundred times—"Our marriage is better today than it ever was. We are so thankful we didn't give up."

Unfortunately, ten months after our separation, the woman who is now my ex-wife filed for divorce. She chose to maintain her relationship with the other man. I learned what many of you reading these words already know: While one person can maintain the hope of rebuilding a marriage, it ultimately takes two to rebuild it.

Maybe you, as I, have gone a divorce you didn't want—even though there were Scriptural grounds for it. I am grateful there was a cross I could move toward in those difficult days, a cross where I could lay all my mistakes and sins, a cross where I found love, forgiveness, and grace.

The same cross that ministered to me is available to minister to you, too. If you have divorced or are just thinking about it—if you had a Scriptural divorce or an unjustified one—start wherever you are, and move toward the cross.

God Starts With People Where They Are

This brings us to our third truth—God starts with people where they are. I've heard of some people who teach that if you're illegitimately divorced and remarried, you have to divorce your present partner and try to get back with your previous partner. Don't do that. You can't unscramble the egg.

In John 4, Jesus talked to a woman who had been married five times and was currently living with a man who was not her husband. But Jesus didn't tell her to go back and marry her first husband again. He started with this woman where she was and moved her toward a relationship with him. He didn't approve of her past actions, but he didn't lock her into her past, either. He gave her hope for her future. He demonstrated that God can take our bad situations and make good come out of them. Her future became brighter. Her whole life was turned around that day. In fact, this woman marked by multiple divorces led a great city-wide revival and brought many others to the Lord.

God always starts with people where they are. If you've divorced for some illegitimate reason, and you know it was wrong, start moving toward the cross today. Jesus said he would receive all who come to him, and that includes the divorced and remarried. When a woman who had been caught in the very act of adultery was brought to Jesus, Jesus told her, "Neither do I condemn you. Go now and leave your life of sin" (John 8:11). He was saying, "I'm going to start with you where you are. You turn away from that life, begin moving toward me, and we'll rebuild your life together."

God wants his family to be a community of "wounded healers." We help each other to rebuild broken lives and recover from dream intruders by the grace that we ourselves have received.

Perhaps you've gone through a divorce, and you're wondering, "How do I rebuild now?" This is the answer: on the foundation of grace in Jesus Christ. I know that sounds trite. But with all of my heart and with great conviction, I believe the only way you can permanently rebuild is to move toward the cross.

I received a letter from a woman who went through a divorce many years ago. She wrote:

> When one loses a loved one because they want to be free from the commitment of marriage. . . . sometimes there are no words to describe the pain in the heart of the abandoned partner. But that's when God carries you in His arms. It happened to me after 10 years of marriage and 2 children. And I can tell you through 42 years of being single, my life was strengthened through living close to the Lord.

I want to tell you something about the Lord's strength. You won't find it coming in great big doses that just make you feel like you can conquer the world. He gives it a day at a time. So just take things a day at a time. Don't worry about the mountain. Don't worry about the future. Focus on today.

"Do not worry about tomorrow, for tomorrow will worry about itself. Each day has enough trouble of its own" (Matthew 6:34). Taking things a day at a time, in the power of the Lord, has got me through more difficulties than you could ever imagine. God is faithful. He will help you each day.

So where does this bring us? **Wherever you are, move toward the cross.**

- If you've just gone through a divorce, remember: wherever you are, move toward the cross.
- If your mom and dad have split up, maybe it was years ago, but you've never really gotten over it. Remember: wherever you are, move toward the cross.
- If your spouse has recently left you, remember: wherever you are, move toward the cross.
- If you've left your mate, and you know it's wrong, it's not too late to work on it. Remember: wherever you are, move toward the cross.

If you'll take the first step toward the cross, Jesus will meet you where you are and help you make the journey the rest of the way. However, to this point, Jesus has done everything he can do. It's up to you to make the next move. Maybe you need to take a quiet moment with him right now and say, "Lord, I've tried to go through life on my own and I'm not going to do it any more. I've learned that my journey without you is meaningless. I need you to walk with me to forgive me, strengthen me, lead me, and give me hope."

You may not notice mountains in your life moving at first. The Lord doesn't always work with dynamite and bull dozers. He likes to start on the inside and work out.

Trust Jesus, the one who has known hurt worse than anything you can imagine. Trust him to make it all come out for something good, when the ugly bandages finally come off. Trust him because he promised he would be there. Trust him—and move toward the cross.

Questions for Discussion

1. The author lists several struggles faced by the divorced. What are they? Which do you think is the hardest to

handle? Why? Which is hardest for non-divorced people to understand or to feel sympathy about? Why?

2. How much should the church attempt to help a divorced person financially? Under what conditions should financial help be available? Why?

3. What can the church or individual Christians do to help the children scarred by divorce?

4. How does the church—or family members, or Christians generally—maintain the balance between acceptance of the *person* but repudiation of the *sin* of divorce? Especially in the case of the guilty (or more guilty) party, how can acceptance be communicated without implying the sin does not matter?

5. The author says, to deal with guilt, a person must "move toward the cross." Whether the person is non-Christian or a Christian, his need is the same. Which of the two do you think is harder to convince of his need to move toward the cross? Why? How can that message be communicated in a positive way?

6. Summarize God's perspective on divorce. Do you believe this ideal is being properly upheld in churches today? By individual Christians? By society? What do you think is the greatest need to reestablish God's standard as the norm?

7. Under what circumstances is divorce "permissible"? Under what circumstances, if any, would you say it is "desirable"? Under what circumstances, if any, would you say it is "required"? What principles guide your answers?

8. The author says Jesus starts with people where they are. How can we start where people are and help them to move closer to the cross?

9. What do you need to do right now to "move toward the cross"? When are you going to do it?